Acclaim for *Follow the Rabbit-Proof Fence*:

"By car it's about 1,300 km. The way Molly Kelly walked … more like 1,600 km. To take the journey is to try to measure the pain that tore Molly Kelly's heart, to trace the scar.

To follow in the footsteps of the Aboriginal woman is to discover one of the least known, but most remarkable, feats of endurance in Australian history; an adventure of great cleverness and courage. It is also to understand something of the scars on the Australian soul."

Tony Stephens, *Age*

"A vividly told story about cultural arrogance, cruelty and courage."

Ian McFarlane, *Canberra Sunday Times*

"This book is almost unbearable to read, and yet is still compulsive. Doris Pilkington is a writer of many skills, and here uses them to tell the extraordinary story of her mother."

Juliette Hughes, *Eureka Street*

"Uncontrived and unadorned, Pilkington's story is genuinely moving."

Debra Adelaide, *Sydney Morning Herald*

"No episode in Australia's history is more ideologically sensitive or of greater contemporary significance for Indigenous and non-Indigenous relations than the story of the Stolen Generations."

Robert Manne, *Sydney Morning Herald*

Comments on the film "Rabbit-Proof Fence":

"It's about the importance of love. About having a heart. About the real people behind the policies and statistics the politicians like to pile up in front of them. It's about giving them names, telling their stories.

That's what Doris Pilkington Garimara had in mind when she wrote down the story of her mother Molly on which the film is based."

Susie Eisenhuth, *Bulletin*

"More Australians will awaken to the cruel reality of the Stolen Generation by watching the 'Rabbit-Proof Fence'. My Nana was taken away from her mother at the age of three. A lot of people still don't quite understand a lot of the emotions, such as the traumas that one experiences when they are taken away from their parents — the separation and the injustice that occurred back in the 1930s in this movie. People who watch this movie will walk away changed more than they may realise."

Cathy Freeman, *Courier-Mail*

"I hope the film will encourage us to reclaim that part of our history for ourselves. It's only by coming to terms with the past, that you can go ahead into the future."

Phillip Noyce, Director of "Rabbit-Proof Fence"

"I could not have written the script without Doris. Without her, it would have been a real outsider's view."

Christine Olsen, Author of "Rabbit-Proof Fence" filmscript

"Sorry, Molly. Sorry, Daisy. Sorry that a book and a movie, inspired by injustice and your bravery, have taken so long to be acknowledged."

Skye Yates, *Daily Telegraph*

DORIS PILKINGTON | NUGI GARIMARA

under the Wintamarra tree

University of Queensland Press

First published 2002 by University of Queensland Press
Box 6042, St Lucia, Queensland 4067 Australia

www.uqp.uq.edu.au

Typeset by University of Queensland Press
Printed in Australia by McPherson's Printing Group

Distributed in the USA and Canada by
International Specialized Book Services, Inc.,
5824 N.E. Hassalo Street, Portland, Oregon 97213–3640

This project has been assisted by
the Commonwealth Government through
the Australia Council, its arts funding
and advisory body.

Sponsored by the Queensland Office
of Arts and Cultural Development.

Cataloguing in Publication Data
National Library of Australia

Pilkington, Doris, 1936–   .
  Under the Wintamarra tree.

  1. Pilkington, Doris, 1936–   . 2. Moore River Native
  Settlement (W.A.) — Biography. 3. Aborigines, Australian —
  Western Australia — Biography. 4. Aborigines, Australian —
  Women — Western Australia — Biography. 5. Aborigines,
  Australian — Western Australia — Removal. 6. Aborigines,
  Australian — Western Australia — Treatment. I. Title.

994.10049915

ISBN 0 7022 3308 0

In memory of my daughter Geraldine
and
granddaughter Akira Jade.

Contents

Acknowledgments

I gratefully acknowledge and thank my mother, Molly Millungga; my aunts Daisy Mudaworra, Keamy Colley Burungu and Mona Burungu (dec.), and Dallas Rose for providing information and sharing their experiences with me; and Arts W.A. and the Council for the Arts for making it possible to research and write this story. And to Louise Glover who joined us on the path to finding the Wintamarra tree and shared in that special event. Special thanks to Edward my partner.

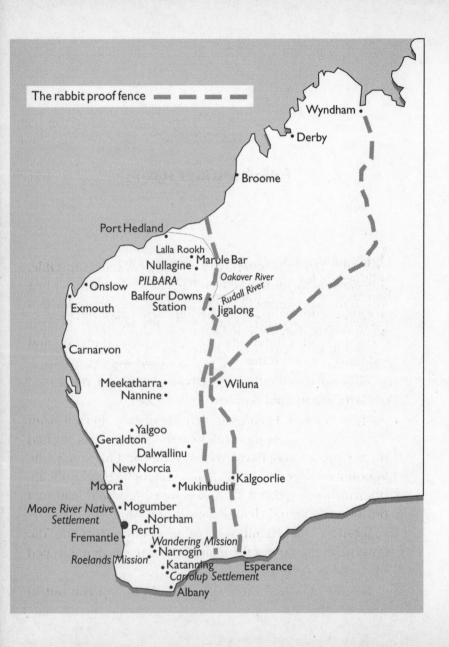

The rabbit proof fence ▬ ▬ ▬ ▬

Wyndham
Derby
Broome
Port Hedland
Lalla Rookh
Nullagine · Marble Bar
PILBARA
Onslow
Balfour Downs
Station
Exmouth
Oakover River
Rudall River
Jigalong
Carnarvon
Meekatharra
Nannine
Wiluna
Yalgoo
Geraldton
Dalwallinu
New Norcia
Kalgoorlie
Moora
Mukinbudin
Moore River Native
Settlement
Mogumber
Northam
Fremantle
Perth
Wandering Mission
Roelands Mission
Narrogin
Esperance
Katanning
Carrolup Settlement
Albany

CHAPTER 1

Leaving the Desert

W HEN THE SUN WAS HIGH and the heat uncomfortable, the Mardudjara women returned to camp, their wirnis filled with wamula. Tjirama Garimara and his sons arrived with a cooked kangaroo and a couple of bungarras to add to their collection. After the meal of kangaroo meat, bungarra and wamula everyone rested, as was the custom.

They woke to shouts coming from the north-east.

"Who's that?" old Bambaru Banaka asked.

"I don't know, I can't see them clearly yet" her husband Tjirama replied. As the group came closer, he recognised them. "It's old man Bayuka, my brother, and his family," he announced happily. As his family watched the visitors approach they could not know this meeting would lead to a decision that would change their lives forever.

Bayuka and his family were on their way to Jigalong, the government depot for the maintenance teams that travelled up and down the rabbit-proof fence.

Bayuka informed them that everything had run out in

their country. There was no food left north of the river.
"We're all starving up there."

Many clans in the region were migrating to Jigalong because their traditional food sources were disappearing. They
were coming to depend on the Government rations from the
depot.

"There's still plenty of food around here," said Tjirama.
"Stay with us tonight and go on early in the morning."

The invitation was gratefully accepted. With the good
rainfall of the past season the desert had blossomed and, for
the first time in a number of years, there was a bountiful
supply of bush food in the Buungul area.

The travels of Bambaru and her family across the desert
were determined by the seasonal changes that affected their
food sources. When food was scarce they survived by eating
small lizards, mice and birds. During the past few weeks there
had been no shortage of food. However, there was still some
concern as yali was fast approaching.

After the evening meal the two families talked well into
the night. During their conversation Tjirama voiced his plan,
"You know Bambaru, we should shift to Jigalong, too."

"Not now," she replied, "there's plenty of food here."

Bambaru was Tjirama's first wife, and the mother of their
daughters Bami Burungu and Togoda Burungu and sons
Balga Burungu, Toby Burungu and Ngidi (last child). Also
in their family group were Mayu Banaka, Tjirama's second
wife, and her sister Mayabinga Millungga. Bambaru was
blind — having lost her sight like many desert dwellers to
trachoma or "sandy blight" — but her memory and knowledge of gathering and preparing bush foods made her

invaluable. As a girl growing up in Buungul around the Rudall River with her family, who moved from camp to camp in search of food in the desert, she learned much about the Gududjara country. She understood the importance of a sound knowledge of the land and imparted much of her wisdom and information to the younger women because she knew it would help to ensure the survival of her children and grandchildren. They were the ones who would practice and preserve the customs of the Gududjara.

The Gududjara and Mandildjara people had lived in harmony with their land for thousands of years and, like other indigenous people, they were practicing conservationists, taking only what was needed. They learned from their ancestral Spirit Beings that if they took care of the land, the land would reciprocate, providing an abundance of plants and game.

This practice of reciprocation and its obligations were upheld, not only by the Gududjara and Mandildjara, but by the Mardudjara people of Jigalong and, further, across the length and breadth of the Western Desert region. This was the unbroken golden thread woven through the fabric of their way of life and it had to be preserved. Bambaru had known harsh conditions in the past and she was prepared to endure worse. Tjirama Garimara, however, had had enough hardship and was in favour of moving closer to the white settlement to escape the uncertainties of food shortages and possible starvation — especially now that his co-wife, Mayu, was expecting their first child.

Tjirama had decided. He ordered his son Balga to go with Bayuka to Jigalong to learn the way there and then come back for his mother, aunties, sisters and Ngidi. Balga protested but his father was determined, so he agreed to accompany his uncle's family.

At sunrise next day, Bayuka Garimara and his family left the camp with Balga and headed for Jigalong Depot.

* * *

The days of dry winds and constant heat were fast approaching, with the roots and seeds of the desert drying up and dust storms almost a daily occurrence. That was bad enough, but what was even more alarming was that this time the water in the soaks and rock holes was drying up quicker than ever before.

Balga returned to his family in the desert and reported that Jigalong seemed a suitable place to shift to. Tjirama made the decision to carry out his plan to move. He knew he must get his blind wife Bambaru and his co-wife, Mayu, to a place with food and, according to Balga, that place was Jigalong. There they would join up with other relations.

He told his family they would all be better off at Jigalong. "Balga will guide you. Toby and I will wait here until he comes back for us, and after he's rested we will follow."

Bambaru agreed at last. "We'll start at sunrise tomorrow."

The long and difficult journey began immediately after the first meal of the day: kangaroo and mayi. Bambaru, Ngidi and the female members of the group made preparations to travel.

Balga led, walking along the riverbank carrying a fire stick and his hunting gear. After a while he left the group to hunt for food. They agreed to meet up later at a well-known soak.

By noon the sweltering heat and burning sand made it

impossible to walk any further. They were glad to reach the soak where they sat down in the shade of a cadgebut tree, waiting for Balga to join them. He arrived carrying a lean, cooked kangaroo. After the meal they rested. Late in the afternoon, the heat decreased and they resumed their their trek towards the depot. They covered many miles and Bambaru, with her hand on the shoulder of Mayu, set a pace to suit them both, keeping rhythm as they followed behind.

Just before nightfall the group made camp, had a quick meal and settled themselves around the small fire. There wasn't much game to be seen in this arid, rocky country. Each night when they lay down to sleep they wondered if the young hunter would be lucky tomorrow. Some days there would be just enough for the morning meal.

Their situation was getting desperate, they were short of food and there was still quite a way to go. The lizards the women caught were really not worth the energy spent search-ing for them as their flesh was barely enough for a taste. Mice were in better condition; however, there were never enough to satisfy the whole group. There was always water to drink so, when there was no meat, at least there was mayi and water to make a simple meal.

Bambaru and her small band of desert nomads followed the Rudall River, across the river flats until they came to the wide spinifex plains scattered with weeping wintamarra and acacia trees. The plains were bounded by large rocky out-crops. The group had to walk around them, adding miles to their trek. Repeatedly the extreme heat would drive them to seek the shade of a tree where they would rest quietly, listening to the cicadas, their shrill noise accompanied by the cawing of the crows, while the heat shimmered across the arid plain. Spurred on by hunger, the family set off again across the spinifex flats as soon as the air cooled down. Their perseverance was rewarded. As the sun was sinking, the tired and hungry group reached the gates of Talawana Station, the most remote station on the edge of the Western Desert.

Except for Balga, none of them had ever seen a station homestead or a white man before. For the first time in their lives they were confronted by fences, a barrier that marked the boundary of a new owner and method of control.

For them, ancestral land was handed down by the Spirit Beings of the Dreamtime and each clan or group knew exactly where the boundaries were and each group respected each other's land. This area around the Rudall River was then and still is known as "the land of the Jilla" and the people as "people of the Rainbow Snake".

These Mardudjara were confused, they didn't know what to do and had no idea how to enter the place. For Bambaru, who could not see it, the fence was described by Mayabinga, her skin-group sister. They looked to Balga for help.

"What now, Son?" asked Bambaru. "What do we do now?"

Balga opened the gate.

"Come on, come this way, follow me. We'll go to Uncle Nalgo Banaka's camp." The group followed nervously.

They were a few yards inside the gate when they saw the strange, pale-skinned man with covering all over his body, sitting on a big, wide-eyed beast and heading straight for them. They had nothing to shield them and nowhere to hide.

"Look out!" yelled Mayabinga. "It might be a marlbu. Get

ready to run!" They formed a tight circle around Bambaru, protecting her from danger.

"No, no," said young Balga. "Don't be frightened, he's the boss." Balga's family stood frozen to the spot, waiting for the stranger to give a command to attack them. But it never came.

The stranger called out to them. They didn't understand the words, and they were too frightened to move. He pointed and following the direction of his hand they could see smoke rising from what looked like camp fires.

Understanding the gestures, Balga nodded politely. "He wants us to follow him," he told the group.

The station owner escorted the weary travellers to the station workers' camps. They walked in single file, Bambaru's hand firmly on her sister's shoulder and Balga in the lead, still carrying his fire stick. The camps were situated far from the homestead, and each family group built their own wuundu made of discarded iron and timber from the station.

That evening the newcomers sat with the station worker families around the fire and were offered their first meal in two days. They held back; station food was new to them. But once they tasted it, they joined in with gusto. There was damper, fresh beef and sweet milky tea. While they feasted, Nalgo attempted to instruct them in the new and different ways of life at their next stop, Jigalong Depot. But judging by their weariness he could see tomorrow would be a more suitable time, after a good night's sleep.

While at Talawana Station Bambaru and her family were informed about the way of life they would experience at Jigalong. Nalgo told them of the depot, which was a cultural crossroads for various Mardu clans and customs, and of the even stranger habits and customs of the whites who lived there.

At last it was time for them to travel the last leg of their long journey to the Jigalong Depot, where they would be reunited with the members of their family who had left the desert some time ago.

Only a month previously, in September 1934, the superintendent of Jigalong, A.T. Hungerford, had written to A.O. Neville, the Chief Protector of Aborigines:

> "I got 5 natives last week, two sick, two old and one man about 25–30. He is from Rudall River and cannot speak a word of English. The blacks seem to look on this place as a depot for all old or sick women with children. Now that the outside waters are drying up, a number of them are coming in from the desert country."
>
> Department of Native Affairs File No. 94/96

Upon their arrival at Jigalong, Bambaru and her family were taken to see Mr Hungerford. Not only was he the superintendent of the depot, Mr Hungerford was also the authorised local Protector of Aborigines. He sent them over to the store to collect rations of food and blankets, and their first taste of tobacco. Usually the boss would give them some white man's clothes to wear, but there were none left in the storeroom.

When the storekeeper, Joe Parker, asked through an interpreter what the little boy's name was, Bambaru responded, "He's just Ngidi, the last child — no name."

"We'll call him Jacky Parker," the storekeeper declared.

So, although he was still referred to as Ngidi, he was called Jacky Barker, the "P" simply replaced with a "B".

Bambaru Banaka, her sisters, daughters and sons were supplied with enough food for a couple of days. After a few days of rest and nourishment Balga and his uncle Robinya Banaka, his mother Bambaru's kinship brother, returned to the desert to bring Tjirama and Toby in to start a new life.

For safety Tjirama took an alternative route to the one Bambaru and the others had taken because he was crossing the territory of other clans, and of land claimed by recent white settlers. Instead of walking through Talawana Station property, Tjirama and Robinya followed the Rudall River to the Oakover River until they reached the boundary fence of Balfour Downs Station.

When they came to Bugina Hill, the men's sacred ceremonial grounds, a few miles north of the station, they made camp. The next morning they lit a fire and threw green gum leaves over it to create smoke, signalling to the station's Mardu workers that they had arrived and were awaiting an escort to enter Balfour Downs.

They waited and after a couple of hours a worker named Ned Garimara arrived riding a black stallion. He brought gifts of food and tobacco. After a drink of warm sweet tea, they set off towards the homestead. Tjirama and his two sons went through what all other Mardu migrants had to endure. Through their interpreter, Ned Garimara, they were ordered to "cover their nakedness". They were introduced to the station owners, the Dunnets, and were allocated jobs around the homestead, which included gardening and chopping wood for the kitchen and laundry. They didn't mind this work, in fact they liked it.

Tjirama was encouraged to remain on the station until "pink-eye" time. This was when all of the station workers had time off to attend their clan's traditional ceremonies. As a Law man Tjirama Garimara realised that there were not many Gududjara and Mandildjara and other Mardudjara people still living in the desert who could uphold the ceremonial traditions and rituals, so together they must create a new Law centre. Ceremonial and sacred objects were moved from their special locations in the desert and buried near the Jigalong Depot. This removal and replacement declared to all the Mardudjara people that this was the new Law centre. From Robinya's information Tjirama learnt that a big meeting for Law Business was to be held in two weeks time. Law time was an important occasion for everyone.

After special secret ceremonies such as the initiation rites, marriages would be announced. Choosing the right ngubas for their offspring was a vital concern for parents. There are four kinship or skin groups — Banaka, Garimara, Burungu, and Millangga. A person is born into one of these groups and cannot change or transfer into another group. A man must choose a wife from the right group to avoid a marriage that would be seen as incestuous and unacceptable to the community. There were stories of couples who eloped only to be apprehended and escorted back to Jigalong to face traditional punishment such as public flogging and ostracism.

Finding suitable wives within the appropriate groups meant that men must be present at the big Law Business meetings at Jigalong where they would have the opportunity to meet their umari and eventually their nguba.

After the Law Business was completed, Tjirama travelled to Jigalong. Now free from the worry of hunger, he and Bambaru Banaka set up their camp on the opposite side of the depot, on the banks of the Jigalong River, to await the birth of Mayu's baby.

CHAPTER 2

Life on Balfour Downs Station

Bambaru and her family settled into life at Jigalong Depot. At neighbouring stations Mardus were employed by the white station owners to work the cattle. Some of Bambaru's relatives had moved to Balfour Downs for work.

When Bill and Mary Dunnet had arrived at Balfour Downs a few years before, they were not well prepared for the harsh life. The Mardu women taught Mary Dunnet, known as "the Missus", how to make bread in a camp or Dutch oven. But when they were short of meat it was the Missus who provided traditional game for her workers, and she became a skilled shooter. The Missus and her Aboriginal workers learned much from each other.

The Dunnets and their partners the Bleachmores found that raising beef cattle was much tougher than the dairy farming they were used to. Coming from the lush green pastures and pristine forests of Margaret River in the south-west, the Dunnets and Bleachmores were confronted with not only the harsh, dry country, but also the lack of personal and home comforts. Managing and adapting to the vast expanses of the grazing lands and the sweltering heat proved too difficult for the Bleachmores. They sold their stake in Balfour Downs to Clarrie Dunnet, Bill's brother.

Bill and Mary Dunnet's daughter Dallas became special to the whole station community. She was born at Meekatharra District Hospital, over 200 miles south of Balfour Downs Station. Her mother never lacked for support and assistance, the Mardu girls and women were willing helpers.

Except for a term at a boarding school, Dallas' education was done through the School of the Air by correspondence course. Each day after school she and the young Mardu girls, who were her companions, would go out riding or walking in the bush. She learned about their traditional foods and the customs of a hunting and gathering society. Her parents did not interfere with the traditional customs of the station families and neither did they prevent Dallas from learning Mardu language or listening to the Dgududani or Dreaming Stories.

Visitors often commented on the station's community atmosphere, based on honesty, trust and sharing of the workload. One day William Henderson, a young Scotsman who had arrived in Australia in the 1930s, came to work for the Dunnets. Initially, he settled in Nannup where he worked for the Hugginses, Mary Dunnet's parents. William was a handsome fellow with blue eyes and curly blond hair. He liked adventure and thrived on challenge, and soon he left the green, well-watered countryside of Nannup to experience life on a remote cattle station. At Balfour Downs he settled into station life and the Dunnets regarded him as a good worker. Mary Dunnet felt some responsibility for him because her mother, Mrs Higgins, wrote regularly to William's mother in Scotland, keeping her up to date with news of her son.

But some, like Dallas, weren't sure how to take him. William's easy manner and good looks made him popular with the young girls who worked at the station homestead. On occasion, Bill Dunnet had to speak to William about chatting to the girls and distracting them from their work.

* * *

The Dunnets and their Mardu workers had a kind of solidarity that was formed on deep loyalties. This, however, did not change the Dunnets' colonialist attitude. The station policy of segregation meant the Mardu workers were never invited to join their boss for a meal at the homestead, instead the workers had their meals outside under the large wintamarra tree, or if it was raining they moved into the bough shed. That wintamarra tree is still referred to today as the midka or eating tree. The homestead staff took trays of food to the workers' families in the camps. These were referred to as the "native" camps and were situated outside the homestead boundary.

The Dunnets were no different from other station owners in the frontier region who maintained white supremacist practises. To many who worked for them the Dunnets were generous and caring bosses whose fairness and consideration worked both ways. They not only expected their Mardu workers to follow Balfour Downs practices but Bill, Mary and Clarrie Dunnet actually took the time to learn about the traditions and customs of the Mardus. As a result the Dunnets knew about the kinship system where avoidance laws were practised and maintained, such as which Mardu were allowed to work together and those whose company other workers must avoid.

The partnership between pastoralists and their Mardu employees was recognised throughout the north-west. The Mardu provided the labour, while their employers were responsible for their welfare. It meant that their employers had to take care of them. For example, the employers were made aware that, under the Native Administration Regulation No. 1–06N(a): "the cost of transporting sick or injured Natives to and from the Protector and/or hospital shall be borne by the employer" (Department of Native Affairs File No. 345/36).

The Dunnets were pleased with their team of station workers, mainly because they worked continuously over a period of time, not just in erratic spurts. This attitude was appreciated because it was through the efforts of the Mardu stockmen and women that Balfour Downs became a thriving cattle station.

Although the Mardu workers were unable to read and write they had the ability and willingness to learn to do any craft or task that station life required. They lived under conditions few white people would willingly tolerate. Most of them were desert nomads and preferred a semi-nomadic life, which meant they needed to move easily when circumstances or ceremonial customs deemed it necessary to shift camp. The Mardu workers and their families shifted camp when there was a death in the family.

One of the major problems on all pastoral stations and depots, which caused frequent confrontation between the

Mardu people and the police (their Protection officers), was the ownership of dogs. The police regularly patrolled the region to record births and deaths, and to carry out other official business. Aboriginal people were not allowed to have more than one unregistered male dog. This legislation was introduced to prevent Aboriginal people from owning and using dogs for hunting, warmth and protection — a subtle way to control their movements and take away their independence, forcing many to leave their traditional homelands to settle on Government depots and to seek employment on pastoral leases.

When the local constable visited Billanooka Station east of Balfour Downs, one particular old woman was always missing. Her name was Stumpy, her "proper" name was Maude Garimara.

Maude had four dogs, two were fearless "jump-in" dogs — effective killers. With them she needed no rifle to hunt for game, her dogs saw that she never went short of meat. When the police constable arrived at the station all Aboriginal workers knew that they had to choose which dogs they wanted to keep. That old Garimara woman didn't want to part with any of her four dogs — she decided to keep all of them.

Maude reared a grandson, Alan, the son of her sister Yowie's daughter, whom she saved from being buried alive by the midwives who delivered him, because he was a muda-muda. Maude also had a muda-muda daughter, Molly Craig, who had been taken from her family as a teenager, but had run away from Moore River Settlement and now lived at Balfour Downs.

Maude and Alan had developed a routine, the boy would climb the tallest tree on the hill and watch until the police constable disappeared from sight. Then the pair would return to the homestead.

But on this occasion a deep gruff voice greeted her, "Hullo Stumpy." Before she could turn around the policeman aimed his pistol and shot two of her dogs in quick succession. He mounted his horse and rode off leaving the distraught old Mardu woman and her grandson to bury the dogs. While Maude was digging the graves she abused the officer in Bududjara, saying he was going to have bad luck and sorrow.

The next day Maude packed their swags and she and Alan moved to Jigalong, following the rabbit-proof fence.

CHAPTER 3

Tree of Life

ON THE CATTLE STATIONS near the Jigalong Depot the Mardu mastered the skills of riding and mustering. Families lived in camps near the station homesteads and the Mardu women went to work on the stations, some as stock workers like the men, and others in the homesteads. There they would carry out domestic chores, cooking and cleaning or caring for the children of the station owners. Some of the girls, like Bambaru's daughter Togoda (who was given the Anglo name Mona), became companions to the station owner's children.

Maude's daughter Molly Craig was one of the Mardus who worked for the Dunnets at Balfour Downs. She was a lively independent woman like her mother. Her fierce independence and determination had already made her known throughout the state. Nine years earlier, as a teenager, she and her two younger cousin-sisters, Gracie Fields and Daisy Burungu, had run away from the Moore River Settlement. They'd been sent there by the Government because their fathers were white, and the Government enforced a policy of removing these children from their Aboriginal families.

Molly and her sisters escaped on foot, using their traditional skills to survive. In a journey that became famous across the country, they followed the rabbit-proof fence from east of Moore River, all the way back to their country, over a thousand miles. During their journey Gracie had been captured at Wiluna and sent back to Moore River, but Molly and Daisy reached Jigalong and moved out into the desert with their families until the Government lost interest.

Daisy had married and moved further south, near Wiluna, with her stockman husband and children. Molly was now a young woman living with some of her family on Balfour Downs and working in the kitchen for the Dunnets. One evening, while the girls were washing up after tea, Bill and Mary heard sudden peals of laughter and giggling coming from the kitchen.

"That sounds like William entertaining the native girls in the kitchen again," said Bill. Such behaviour raised concern but the Dunnets decided it was innocent fun.

William Henderson left Balfour Downs one day without explanation and returned to Nannup where he drove a truck for the Brunswick Creamery.

Several months later, on a hot summer afternoon when the tall wintamarra trees were casting long shadows across the red, stony earth, Molly was resting quietly outside her camp. Suddenly her peaceful thoughts were interrupted by the boss.

"Molly, you want to come out riding with us?" he asked, pointing to the other four station workers riding with him. Molly had been out working the cattle the previous day.

"No, I don't feel too good," she replied, touching the right side of her abdomen. "I got 'pendix again." Molly had previously suffered several attacks of appendicitis.

"Alright Molly," he called out. "You stay home and rest."

"Yes Boss," she said softly. As she watched the riders gallop away through the gates she decided to have a rest. She stood up and rubbed her lower back, shook out her dusty blankets and spread them evenly over the coconut fibre mattress. Then she settled down to rest. Her wuundu had its own fire, and she and her eight-year-old cousin-sister Daisy slept under the stars at their camp.

But sleep eluded Molly so she sat up and focused her eyes on the blue hills to the right of the camp, Bugina and Jilla worro, the men's secret sacred place where most of the men were now, including her nguba, Toby Burungu.

The two gardeners Riley and Dodger and her brother-in-law Balga Burungu remained at the station to carry on with the chores that were required. This year the Law Business meeting was being held over there in the blue hills. There were ten initiates and they would be in the camp for a long time. Only yesterday the boss took a killer (a carcass of beef) to them.

"He's a good man, that Mr Dunnet," thought Molly. She felt another pain in her lower back. "I shouldn't have lifted that big bag of flour by myself, I must've hurt myself," she muttered.

She was feeling restless and unable to settle down. She glanced at Daisy, who was playing in the shade with some knucklejacks which had been passed on from Dallas, the Dunnet's daughter. Pointing to the stockyards, Molly said softly, "That smell is strong this afternoon."

"Yes, it's strong all right," Daisy replied without taking her eyes off the knucklejacks. It was a typical December day, the heat intense, and an afternoon breeze carried the smell of cattle manure across the stony gibber flats towards their camp.

"Nobody here to clean it up and take it away," said Molly as she tried once more to rest. She gave up, and decided to prepare the evening meal for herself and Daisy.

The boss and his stock workers returned home as the sun was sinking low. It was a typical, beautiful Pilbara sunset with bright orange, red and golden clouds that stood out on a background of pink-tinted shades between a sky of blue and clouds of wispy grey. No two sunsets were the same, their beauty was something to admire, but mostly it was something people took for granted. On that December evening neither Molly or Daisy showed any interest in the sunset.

"I wish the doctor would do something about this 'pendix," Molly said out loud.

"What's the matter, Dgudu?" asked her young cousin-sister.

"I'm sick of this pain," Molly said as she rubbed her stomach. In a few minutes the pain was gone. "That's better, we can have some supper now."

The two sisters ate their meal in silence. Molly was hoping that there would be no more pain that night as she was feeling very tired and needed a good night's sleep, so she stretched out on her bed and tried to relax as she waited for sleep to overtake her weary body.

In the stillness of the night Molly let her thoughts wander

back to last year's Law Business meeting when she was given a nguba. His name was Balga Burungu, but he had a choice of two Millungga women and chose Mousie Millungga, and Molly was passed on to Toby Burungu, his brother. Molly protested but she was reminded by her mother Maude that she must marry this Gududjara man from Rudall River and be the "right" way this time. Molly never told the Missus about this marriage arrangement.

Mrs Dunnet would prefer Molly to "better" herself and marry a hard-working half-caste man like Andy Everett, who was not only a top horse breaker but one of the best riders in the district. Molly remembered Andy Everett for his tenderness and love for her. He was her first love but unfortunately was also a suitor for the hand of a Yamatji girl from the south.

Molly knew Mrs Dunnet would be very disappointed if she got involved with one of the Mardu men that the Missus referred to as "desert natives".

Terms applying to mixed ancestry, such as half-caste, were in everyday usage in that era. To the Government they were actual terms used to classify people of Aboriginal ancestry and therefore control their destiny.

Molly was still finding it difficult to sleep, so she got up and went to the toilet. "Must be drinking too much water and tea," she thought. On her return to the camp, despite the warmth of the evening, she stoked up the dying embers of the fire. Soon the fire was burning brightly and the heat gave some relief for her aching back.

She gazed around at the other camps nearby. She was the only person awake at that hour. It was past midnight and she felt so alone, standing beside the fire. Suddenly Molly felt a strong pain low in her abdomen. She sat down on her bed and said softly to herself. "Oh no, it can't be." But once she realised what was happening to her, Molly calmly picked up her bedding and bundled together a few things she would need — a knife, some calico. She called quietly to Daisy. "Wake up. Quickly now, we must shift camp over there." Molly pointed to the lone wintamarra tree silhouetted in the moonlight.

"What's wrong, Dgudu?" asked Daisy, still sleepy.

"I want you to help with the baby," said Molly.

"What baby?" asked Daisy, suddenly wide-awake.

"My baby, it's coming soon," hurriedly explained the anxious mother-to-be.

"Can't be," said the innocent young child.

No one had any idea, not even Molly, that she was expecting a baby. She had to think quick — normally the birthing place would have been planned. Together she and Daisy set out for the wintamarra tree. There they spread out their bedding on the ground, preparing a birthing place well away from the camps, as was the tradition of all the Mardu women before them.

Molly relaxed while Daisy's small hands massaged her stomach. Daisy watched closely as the tiny baby was delivered.

"Right, you can cut 'em now," said Molly.

"Cut 'em what?" asked the frightened child.

"All clear now," Molly assured her young assistant. "You can cut 'em off wanna now."

"What am I gunna cut 'em with, Dgudu?" Daisy asked trembling with fear.

"Cut it with that knife," said Molly pointing to a large
butcher's knife that was with the bundle of things she'd
brought from their camp.

"No, that baby little one, too small," said the eight-year-
old. "I might cut it and kill 'im," she added as she moved
away to the other side of the wintamarra tree.

"You won't kill it," assured Molly.

"No Dgudu, don't make me cut 'em wanna," pleaded
Daisy, crying softly in the now cool early morning. "I don't
want to kill your baby."

"Marta! Marta!" she said impatiently. "I'll do it myself."

Daisy, very reluctantly, handed the large knife to her sister,
and quickly turned her back on mother and baby. But curiosity got the better of her, she turned her head slightly then
raised her hands to cover her eyes. Still trembling, she
peeped through her fingers. She expected to see the tiny
baby covered with blood, bleeding from a wound inflicted by
the big sharp knife. The panic-stricken girl sighed with relief,
for there on the blanket was the smallest baby — and the first
half-caste baby — she had ever seen. She was pleased to see
that the wanna had been cut and was tied neatly with a clean
strip of calico.

"You can go back to sleep now," Molly told her. "Everything alright."

Daisy didn't need to be told a second time. Moving quickly
she lifted her rugs and slid underneath, then covered her
head and shut her eyes tightly hoping that sleep would take
over. But every time she closed her eyes the image appeared
of the small new-born baby lying motionless, looking like a

tiny skinned rabbit. It was almost sunrise when Daisy was able to relax and drift off into a peaceful sleep.

The next morning she was awakened by the cawing of half a dozen crows perched on the branches of the wintamarra tree and the chirping and twittering of small birds that were darting in and out of the acacia bushes. She sat bolt upright in her bed, then got up and quietly approached her older sister's bed, touching her gently on the shoulder.

"Dgudu, you 'wake?" Daisy whispered. Molly didn't move, she was sleeping heavily.

"Dgudu, where's the baby?" she persisted, still confused yet curious. Daisy moved slowly to the edge of the bedding, and looked upon the sleeping babe. She was wrapped in calico, lying in the shallow hole her mother had scooped out of the warm earth, as was the tradition in sheltering the newborn.

"Dgudu, this baby weak one, he crying alright, but I can't hear him," said the frightened little girl. "Dgudu, he got no wind," Daisy stared at the baby's chest. "He go 'uh, uh'." She could see that the baby couldn't breath and couldn't cry, was just producing a feeble whimper.

"This skinny baby gunna die," she decided as she leaped up and ran as fast as she could to Peter Balga Burungu's camp shouting loudly, "Brother, Brother! Bakala! Bakala! (Hurry up! Come quickly!)" Then she began to cry.

"What's wrong, wandi?" he answered, standing up quickly and spilling his tea.

"Dgudu got little one baby," she said. "She had 'em in the night."

"Can't be true," Balga said in disbelief. "My brother didn't know that his nguba was a carrier (pregnant)."

"Yes, she have a really little baby and he got no wind, and he got crooked legs," she waffled on then began to cry. "Brother Balga you gotta come and fix 'em up and make 'em better." Then Daisy wailed loudly, "Oh, Oh! He gunna die."

Balga was already striding out across the spinifex flat towards the birthing place to see what had happened.

Daisy suddenly remembered that the baby needed something to sleep in. She spied a half-finished coolamon someone had been carving from an oval-shaped piece of wood. "This will do," she thought, picked it up and ran to catch up to her kinship brother.

When she reached the camp Balga was already massaging the thin tiny legs of his niece. "Brother, can we use this wirni to carry this little one in?" Daisy stood wide-eyed and amazed to see this tiniest newborn child alive and moving.

"I'm not going to let this special baby die," Balga promised Molly as he ever so gently touched his premature niece. Her mother wasn't too sure.

"The baby came too soon, not the proper time." Daisy reminded her brother. "Dgudu lose 'em babies before." She was speaking of the two babies Molly had lost in early term.

"Yes, I know but I'm not letting this baby die," said Balga as he straightened what must be the smallest legs that he'd ever seen. "This child could have been mine, but I chose Mousie as my nguba instead, this is my brother's daughter."

Balga rubbed the infant's scrawny but warm body until he was satisfied that his niece–daughter had a good chance of surviving. Then Balga returned to his camp where Mousie

Millungga was waiting with her mother-in-law Bambaru for news of the latest station baby.

Molly carried her new-born baby back to her camp. She set about lining the coolamon with calico, then placed her baby in the bowl that was to be her cradle. She was still feeling unwell, but that didn't stop her from carting water which she heated over the fire for a quick sponge bath, a task she and young Daisy did every morning before they went to work at the homestead.

Molly decided that she wasn't going to work today, she'd stay and look after the baby. After she dressed she sat on an upturned kerosene drum outside her camp in the warm sunshine.

When Daisy went to check on the baby she was horrified to find that she had fallen out of the lop-sided bowl and was lying on the ground, her tiny face covered in red dust. Alarmed and panic stricken, and without saying anything to her sister, Daisy ran as fast as she could over to the homestead, shouting as she ran, "Missus Dunnet, Missus Dunnet! Quick, Molly chuck 'em baby on the bunna."

"Slow down Daisy. What baby are you talking about?" asked Mrs Dunnet.

"Baby got bunna everywhere," repeated Daisy. "He on the bunna."

"Whose baby's on the ground?" Mrs Dunnet asked her once again, a look of surprise on her face. After all, she knew everyone's business on the station.

"Molly's roan (own) baby. She had 'em in the night," Daisy said. "Born in the camp."

"What!" exclaimed Dallas, "Molly had a baby?"

"Come on," Mary urged her daughter as they rushed down to Molly's camp. They found her still sitting on the drum, staring at the ground, still in shock from the unexpected ordeal.

"Molly, you naughty girl, pick this baby up, now," ordered Mrs Dunnet, as she bent down to touch the new-born child.

"Oh Mum, look at this tiny baby," said Dallas in disbelief. The baby was the smallest she had ever seen. "The poor little thing," she said, her eyes fixed on the little form lying before her, "the crows could have picked her eyes out."

"What a dreadful thought, yet it could easily have happened," agreed her mother. "Molly, you and the baby will stay at the house, you know — the room where the dogger and the 'roo shooter stay," said Mrs Dunnet. Molly nodded as she began to lift the baby back into the wooden bowl.

"No, don't put her in that thing. It's too hard," ordered her boss. "I'll find something more suitable for her." So she dashed up to the homestead and returned with a shoebox filled with cotton wool. That became the baby's incubator.

All four, the three women and Daisy, walked silently back to the house. Daisy followed Mrs Dunnet and Molly into the kitchen then said happily, "I wash 'em baby now."

"What," cried the startled Mrs Dunnet, "you want to wash this tiny baby?"

"Yes Missus, I can wash 'em," she replied confidently.

Molly was horrified. "You can't wash the baby. Don't touch it, you'll break his hands and legs. No, don't touch 'em. I'll wash the baby myself."

"I agree with Molly," said Mrs Dunnet. "Daisy, you can't

handle the baby, it's too small and besides, you're too young."

Daisy was disappointed that she couldn't wash her newly born niece. But she understood why — the infant was too skinny and too small. "It's because he born too soon," Daisy said. She observed with great interest, marvelling at the fully formed, tiny human being cleaned with cotton wool sponges.

Nestled on a bed of cotton wool in a size twelve shoebox, the baby was given her first drink of milk through an eye dropper like a bird.

"What is the baby's name, Molly?" asked Mrs Dunnet.

"Her name is Nugi," the young mother pronounced.

"Nugi, that's a stupid name," said her employer. "Give her a proper name, call her Doris," she ordered.

So little Nugi Garimara became known to the Department of Aboriginal Affairs as Doris Craig, the daughter of "Molly the Half-caste" of Balfour Downs Station. As Doris's birth was unregistered she was later issued by the Department of Native Affairs with the birth date of 1 July 1937, in line with the Government practice of the day.

* * *

A week later the station community had recovered from the shock of the unexpected birth of baby Doris. The tiny premature infant slept peacefully in her shoebox incubator, unaware of the rumour and speculation circulating about her paternity.

Up at the homestead the Dunnets also discussed the issue. The Missus was keen to find out who was the father of Molly's child. She usually knew what was going on around the station, yet she hadn't even known Molly was pregnant. Clarrie thought it might be William Henderson, the good-looking young Scotsman who'd worked at Balfour Downs. But they could not be certain.

While the concerns regarding the parentage of baby Doris were being discussed behind closed doors at the station homestead, in the camps there was no doubt who the baby's father was. But to anyone else, because the child's skin wasn't black, it was assumed that she had a white father.

The Commissioner of Native Affairs was duly notified of the premature baby's birth by Dr Albert Davis, who reported that the baby was too weak and feeble and, according to his expert opinion, would only survive for one week.

The Commissioner wanted further information. "It was suggested to me by Constable Liddlelow, late of Nullagine, that a white man named William Henderson might be the father of the child. Acting on this information I approached Henderson but he denied parentage."

It was his department's policy to remove children of mixed parentage as quickly as possible before the child could be accepted as a member of the community and identify with traditional ways and teachings. As official guardian of half-caste infants, the Commissioner was also determined to take proceedings against Henderson to secure payment of main-tenance as the Department would take Doris into one of its institutions — depending on her skin colour.

"However," the Commissioner wrote, in a letter addressed to the Under Secretary for Law, "before initiating proceed-ing I would be pleased to have the advice of the Law Officers on the likely result of the case as set forth at page 13.

Personally, I think the evidence is sufficiently corroborative
to obtain an order."

A reply from the Crown Prosecutor Mr Sydney Wood to
the Commissioner on 30 April stated that "the corroborative
evidence referred to on page 13 of this file appears to be the
following:

1. The child bears a resemblance to Henderson. This I am
    afraid is too nebulous to be regarded as a material fact.
2. That Henderson was once seen in very compromising
    position with the girl. No date is given either of this
    occasion or of the day of birth and in consequence no
    inference can at present be drawn from it.
3. That as soon as Henderson knew that the girl was to have
    a child he left the station. Lower down in the Policeman's
    report, however, there was a statement that Henderson
    was dismissed so the effect of the previous observation is
    nullified. In any case it is scarcely a corroboration of a
    material fact in the girl's story."

The Crown Prosecutor advised the Commissioner that,
due to insufficient evidence to corroborate Molly's story, he
suggested that Henderson be interviewed again to see
whether he would make some admission or show by his
conduct that he acknowledged paternity.

But William Henderson could not be contacted so the
Commissioner of Native Affairs wrote to Bill Dunnet at
Balfour Downs in May 1938, requesting his assistance in the
matter.

"I would be pleased to learn of the date which you found
Henderson and Molly in a compromising position and which
I understand was one of the reasons why he was dismissed

from your employ." The Commissioner referred to Constable Liddelow's report when Liddelow was visiting the station in February 1936. "He heard you inform Henderson that he must not play with the house girls, one of whom was Molly. Also, was Henderson at any time suspected of association with other native Women?"

Two months later came the reply regarding William Henderson and Molly Craig of Balfour Downs Station.

"Firstly I wish to say that Constable Liddelow has misinformed you when he says that Henderson's association with native women was partly the reason for his dismissal, he left of his own accord and at no time did I have reason to suspect him of association with black women. I did have reason to speak to him when Constable Liddelow was at the homestead about playing with the native girls and stopping them from finishing their work and making a noise in the kitchen.

I am afraid I can not help you any further in this matter, and quite understand Henderson not being willing to shoulder the responsibility when he knew that Molly had native boyfriends at the same time."

By the time the actual particulars were received it was too late for the Department to take any action. The Commissioner advised Bill Dunnet that "whenever a child is born and where there is a suspicion that it may be half-caste, we should at once make inquiries."

When Australia declared war on Germany in September 1939, before the month ended more than 14,000 men had joined the three services — the navy, army and air force. William Henderson was one of them. He joined the infantry and served overseas but never returned to Australia. William

Henderson was captured and imprisoned, he died on the island of Crete.

* * *

Under the supervision of Mary Dunnet, and the growing confidence of her young mother, Doris the premature baby thrived and soon grew too big for her shoebox. "We'll have to find something more suitable," pointed out Mrs Dunnet.

Help came sooner than she anticipated when later, during the cool of the afternoon, she heard loud banging coming from the shed. This wasn't unusual, as Bill was always making and building useful objects for the homestead.

"I wonder what he's making this time?" she said. "He's making a lot of noise."

"That's the boss, Missus," announced Daisy, who was always in attendance. "He making a cradle for baby Doris."

"Making a cradle, how?" Mrs Dunnet inquired.

"Your new copper, Missus," she answered cheerfully.

"What!" yelled Mary Dunnet as she rushed down to the shed, fuming. She couldn't believe it — her new copper — what next? "A cradle from my brand new copper — one that I haven't even used," she said furiously. But when she reached the shed she was pleasantly surprised.

"Do you like it?" asked her husband caressing the timber frame that held the shiny new copper cradle. Mary couldn't help but be impressed with his handiwork.

"I like it very much," she said as she rocked it. "No baby has a better cradle than this one. But" she reminded him, "that was my new copper."

"I know. I'll order another one for you, it will be delivered on the next mail run," he promised. "Come on," he said, carrying the copper cradle back to the homestead where Doris was sleeping. "Let's try it out." But first, Mary made a mattress cover for it from some calico material and filled it with cotton wool. When it was finished the infant was transferred from the shoebox to the cradle.

Daisy, Doris's young aunt, loved to stand and rock the cradle while singing songs like "When the Red, Red Robin" and "The Red River Valley", and other popular songs of the 1930s and 40s that she learned by listening to the Dunnet's gramophone records. These same songs were sung by her niece later on — no nursery rhymes for that little girl!

Doris was a contented baby who grew fast and healthy. The infant's progress was followed with interest by all the members of the station community. When she became too big for the cradle the next stage was to bring Dallas's old cot from the store room.

"We can't have baby Doris falling out of the cradle now, can we?" said Mrs Dunnet.

"No Missus," chorused the domestic staff gathered around to watch Doris's move from the cradle into the cot.

Everyone was delighted when she took her first steps. It was at this time that Doris and Molly moved back to the camp with Toby, living together as a family. Doris became a familiar sight in and around the homestead, often following her father Toby as he worked at his other job, vegetable gardener to the station. From the infant stage of her life she loved pretty things.

One day while toddling around the yard Doris spied the other garden, Mrs Dunnet's colourful flower garden. She headed straight for the bright flowers and plucked a handful.

She took them into the homestead, as she had seen her father do with the freshly picked vegetables, and offered them to Mrs Dunnet.

"Nanna, look at the pretty flowers," said the happy child.

"You naughty little girl," yelled Mary as she snatched the bouquet from her hands and tossed it into the rubbish bin. "You must not pick my flowers from the garden."

The confused toddler was picked up roughly, smacked soundly on the bottom and dumped into a cot.

"Mummy," she cried out, "stop this Grandma from hurting me." But her mother never came. Doris realised that it was useless calling for help because no one would come to her aid. She called out in her Mardu grandmother's language, the Gududjara dialect, and cried herself to sleep.

After that incident Doris never went close to the flower garden again. She learnt a very important lesson that day, a lesson that she never forgot, and that was that she must never touch the plants in the homestead garden, because they were there to admire but not to take.

The incident was soon forgotten, there were other interesting things to see and touch, and one of Doris's favourite places was the vegetable garden where she spent the time with her father Toby and her uncle Balga. She accompanied them when they picked the big ripe, red tomatoes and other vegetables for the homestead kitchen, where meals were prepared for the workers and their families.

One day when the Dunnets were away and her parents were in charge, looking after the homestead, Doris explored beyond the garden and was badly bitten by one of the station's cattle dogs. Her father took the rifle used for kangaroo hunting and shot the dog. Afterwards, anyone who asked where the dog had gone was told it was dead, run over by a truck. To Doris's father, the possibility of the dog attacking again was too great to risk.

CHAPTER 4

Bambaru's Eyes

WHEN JACKY BARKER (Nigdi) was about seven or eight years, his mother Bambara Banaka decided to join her husband Tjirama and her other sons at Balfour Downs Station. Because she was blind her youngest son Jacky was given the job of leading her about. He wasn't a willing guide.

It was mustering season and Jacky wanted to join his older brothers Peter Balga and Toby Burungu.

"You can't ride without wearing boots," the boss reminded him, "That's the policy of the station," he said firmly. "We don't want you getting your feet hooked in the stirrups."

The boy was given the smallest boots in the store, a size two, elastic-sided pair of riding boots, and Mrs Dunnet made him a pair of long pants. So off he went with the mustering team to learn how to be a good rider like his brothers. It didn't matter if the boots were slightly big and loose, he kept them on, and the stirrups had to be pulled up near his knees: he was a stockman, a young cattle man, a worker on the station.

The first mount he was given was a mule, and he wasn't

pleased with that decision at all. "I'm not riding that mule again, and I'm not going mustering with you two," he told his brothers. But he still cried loudly when the team rode out to the mustering camps without him.

One day the boss gave him an old station horse that was his, and only his, to ride. That was ever so much better.

When the mustering of the cattle ended, the boss concluded that Jacky would never be as good as his older brothers. "He's too fat and a very rough rider, and he doesn't have the style and skills like the other youngsters. And besides, Jacky Barker doesn't look good on a horse," he told Jacky's two brothers, "not like you two."

Whether he liked it or not Jacky was needed by Bambaru to guide her from place to place. Everyone knew that he resented being his mother's eyes. Some days he would torment her, leading her into the unused charcoal pit and leaving her there while he went off to play. After a while Bambaru would start shouting for help.

"Nidgi, come here and take me out of this place," and, when there was no response the poor old woman would cry out louder. "Somebody, anybody come and help me," she would cry as she walked around in the pit with both hands feeling along the sides. Jacky continued playing, ignoring his mother's pleas for help.

He would take his mother for a walk and leave her standing by herself in the middle of the gibber flats where she would wander aimlessly, calling for help. Jacky refused to respond to her frantic calls for deliverance from her plight. Sometimes he would be insensitive and inconsiderate and run her through a clump of windamarra trees where the branches hung low and stung her face.

He moved very quickly when ordered by his older brothers and so many times was threatened by them that every day the station community would wonder if he would get his flogging today or not. Everybody agreed that Jacky deserved a good hiding — he came close but he was never punished by his brothers. They just reminded him that while everybody was out working he had to take care of his blind mother.

Everybody was pleased when Jacky did not return with his family from their summer holidays, which they spent at the Jigalong Depot and where he remained. So another lad called Paddy Garimara became Bambaru's minder until her two-and-a-half-year-old granddaughter Doris became her eyes. A special bond developed between them instantly and, unlike her young uncle Jacky Barker, Doris enjoyed Bambaru's company. She had heard talk of the old lady and knew her name meant "the blind one". But at first little Doris couldn't understand why her grandmother couldn't see, because Bambaru's eyes were open.

When her parents went droving cattle to the Meekatharra railhead she was happy to stay with her grandmother until they returned. The young aunts were also there to keep an eye on both of them.

When her mother became pregnant Doris spent all her time with Bambaru. Their relationship grew and developed daily. Even for one so young, Doris seemed to realise Bambaru needed a guide and carer.

Sometimes Bambaru would sit the child on her lap and

touch her soft curly hair, and recall how concerned everyone had been when they saw how tiny the newborn Doris was.

It was the same picture Mrs Dunnet had of her when Doris came up to the homestead. She remembered vividly the day when Doris was almost a week old and Dr Albert Davis visited the station. When he examined the scrawny premature baby he had announced that the child would not survive another week. Who would have thought that the same infant, who weighed only three pounds at birth, would thrive and develop into a healthy happy little girl?

Doris's sharp eyes became useful when Bambaru hunted kangaroos. With two excellent "jump-in" dogs Bambaru and her sister Minda, Keamy's mother, joined forces. Both owned hunting dogs. They had a special but simple plan. While the young girls chased the kangaroos towards them, they waited behind the acacia shrubs with the four dogs until the kangaroos were near. "Now, Bambaru," Doris would whisper, and her grandmother would let the dogs loose for the kill.

The dogs chased the kangaroos until they caught and killed them. Minda skinned and gutted them while the girls collected wood and made a huge fire on the sand in a gully nearby.

The women and girls sat under the shade of the eucalyptus trees and shared station gossip and stories while they waited for the fire to burn so that the coals could be raked into the holes prepared for cooking. When there were sufficient coals lining the bottom of the small pits, the kangaroos were dropped into them, then covered with hot ashes and sand, and left to cook slowly. At last the meat was cooked but only one kangaroo was shared among the small party of female hunters, the other kangaroo would be cut into portions to be divided amongst those back in the camps.

This was the most satisfying part of hunting. Doris and Bambaru shared a tail between them, accompanied by lukewarm milky sweet tea and hot damper. By late afternoon the hunters returned to camp and rested until supper time.

* * *

Doris was a familiar sight as she wandered around the homestead or visited relations in their camps. If she wasn't minding her grandmother Bambaru Banaka, she was playing with other children, who were mostly relatives from Jigalong Depot. She looked forward to having new playmates — especially if they were the same age or younger, then she could be the one to decide what games they should play.

One day her young aunts Kathleen Millungga, Dada Millungga and their brother Jackson Millungga came for a visit with their parents. They pretended to go hunting for murrundus and returned with half a dozen pula-pulas. Doris cooked them and offered them to her uncles and aunts — who protested loudly to their dgudu Molly.

"What's wrong with you?" said her mother, "give them to the dogs!"

It was a long time before the Millungga trio returned to visit Balfour Downs Station.

In time Doris realised that she could control the movement and activities of her grandmother, and this attitude often got them into difficulties. Bambaru allowed herself to be manipulated and persuaded to fulfil Doris's childish impulses and whims.

One day Bambaru was led from the camp by Doris to

search for and dig mata. The pair stayed longer than expected, so when the billy can of water was empty Bambaru
called out loudly for help. No one answered, so she continued yelling until her eldest son Balga Burungu heard her
calls for help and brought a bucket of water for them.

He was so angry that his brother and sister-in-law could
allow this to occur, they were severely reprimanded. "What's
wrong with you?" he said. "They could have perished down
there."

However, one thing Doris did understand was the danger
of aeroplanes. During the war planes were often seen and
heard flying to and from Perth and Darwin. Her aunts had
told her about aeroplanes and how the pilot or "Japani man"
would shoot down at them. One day Doris was playing a few
feet from where her grandmother was resting when she
heard the drone of an aeroplane. In fear and panic the child
rushed over to Bambaru, urging her to get up.

"What's wrong, my little granddaughter?" the old lady
asked sleepily.

"Quick, hurry up Bambaru, get up," said Doris urgently.
She clasped her grandmother's hand in her small one then
led the blind old woman towards the thick acacia bushes and
the tall wintamarra trees. As they passed under the trees the
branches, high enough for little Doris to pass safely beneath,
stung Bambaru's face. She cried out, "Don't go so fast,
Dorissy, the branches are hurting me."

"But they can see us!" Doris replied, pulling her faster. She
found a safe place behind a large boulder and tried to hide
her grandmother there.

Still not satisfied that the "Japani man" couldn't see to

shoot them, she sat protectively in front of her grandmother. When the planes were out of sight the two of them returned to their camp. This action meant so much to Bambaru Banaka that it formed an even stronger bond between her and little Doris.

Doris entertained her grandmother by singing the songs she had learned at the homestead, such as "Bye, Bye, Black Bird" and "Red River Valley".

* * *

There was never a dull moment when Mona Burungu, Bambaru's youngest daughter and one of Doris's young aunts, was around, she always found something to amuse all the young girls. This particular day she decided to take her mother's dogs out hunting for game.

"That's good," said her brother Toby, "you might bring us some meat."

When the girls — Mona, Dinah Millungga, Keamy Burungu and Daisy — reached the hunting grounds, each one took their places ready for the chase. Mona ordered her kinship sisters to flush the kangaroos out of the scrub. A kangaroo leaped out. The dogs, urged on by the girls, gave chase, unaware that a fox startled by the barking dogs had taken refuge in the same bushes. When the dogs sighted the fox they forgot the kangaroo and pursued the fox. It ran towards Mona.

"Worrah!" she yelled. "This fox think I tree. Worrah, worrah!" The other girls ran to her aid. The fox perched on the top of Mona's head; her legs shook uncontrollably, she couldn't keep still.

"Mummy, Mummy, come here and help me," she cried,

her whole body shaking with fear. Mona felt the blood trickling from her head, down her face and into her eyes. This made her cry even louder. "Take this fox off my head!"

Her three kinship sisters picked up long sticks and began hitting the dogs. While the dogs were distracted Keamy lashed out at the fox which leaped off Mona's head, sped off and disappeared into the thick kurrara bushes.

Mona and Keamy returned to Bambaru's camp where Doris was playing under the shady trees. Her brother and sister-in-law tried not to laugh when they were told of the incident, but they could imagine the fox sitting on top of Mona's head.

Seeing the dry blood on her auntie's face Doris became very concerned, but she relaxed when her parents assured her that everything was alright. It was a long time before she had the courage to go hunting again.

* * *

As Doris grew older she wanted to join her young kinship aunties when they went out gathering bush tucker. Her aunts Mona, Dinah, Keamy and Daisy usually told her she was too little, and that they would be going a long way from the station.

Quite often she would run crying to her grandmother Bambaru, who would comfort her by saying "Never mind, you stay with me. You don't want to go with your stupid aunties."

One day, after she stopped crying and was resting her head on her grandmother's breast, she heard them calling her. They had changed their minds. "Come on, hurry up," they chorused.

Doris ran off happily as fast as her little thin legs could go. "I'll bring plenty of mata for you", she promised.

"Alright," called Bambaru. "Now you girls look after my Dorrissy."

They searched around in the most likely places and found quite a few mata. All the girls including Doris were concentrating on digging for yams. Then all of a sudden sounds other than birds and insects were heard some distance away. A deep mumble and bellowing told them a herd of cattle was heading their way. All eyes were focused in the direction of the sound and all watched quietly.

Then at last they saw the cattle — it was a stampede. Mona grabbed her niece's hand and ran towards the nearest wintamarra tree. Once she was safely on a branch she tried to pull Doris up beside her, but it was too late. The small wintamarra tree was swaying from side to side, the branches weighed down by the weight of the other girls.

Closing her eyes tight, Mona began to cry. "Mummy, Mummy," her whole body was shaking with fear. Little Doris joined in crying for her parents.

"Oh shut up you two, we're frightened too but we're not crying," said Dinah.

When the cattle disappeared over the horizon in a cloud of dust the girls climbed down from the tree, still shaking. They decided to return home where they rested quietly in their camps for the rest of the day.

Several weeks later, the same aunties were ordered to take their niece with them for a walk.

"You're a little nuisance," the aunts told Doris, "You should stay home and look after Bambaru."

"No," Doris replied defiantly, "I'm coming with you."

They decided to go in the opposite direction this time, making sure that they were well out of the cattle trail. They sat on the top of a sand dune and watched from a safe distance as the drovers and cattle passed by leaving behind a great cloud of red dust.

An old Mardu man dismounted from his fine-looking black stallion and approached the girls. He sat down in front of Mona and began to cry. Then, as is the custom, she cried with him. Crying is an important part of the Pilbara Aboriginal culture: you cry when a loved has died, you cry for those who have passed away during your absence and you cry as you meet or greet a relative whom you haven't seen for a while. Then the old man left and the mustering team rode on out of sight. Because he was a stranger the other girls asked, "Who was that old man? Where does he come from?"

"I don't know who he was," replied Mona. "He cry for me so I cry for him."

"You're a proper stupid girl," said Daisy as she stood up and started to walk back to the station. The others followed behind. Mona decided it would be much quicker if she piggy-backed her niece instead of expecting her to walk home.

A couple of days later the aunts were off on another adventure. Once again their pesky niece wanted to join them, in fact Doris demanded that they take her along. "Not this time," said her youngest aunt Keamy.

"Mummy," yelled Mona, "keep Doris with you today, we're going through rough country to hunt for murrundu," added her daughter.

"We'll take you next time, alright," promised Mona.

"Alright," replied Doris sulkingly. She knew that she had no choice. She plonked herself down on her grandmother's lap and sulked until her mother came home from the homestead kitchen carrying a tray of food for their lunch. Bambaru loved her only grandchild and knew that she was a special little girl. The little toddler brightened her lonely dark days.

Meanwhile Doris's young aunts were sitting in a dry creek bed discussing station gossip and trying to decide what to do next, "I know," said Mona. "Let's sing and dance."

"What song will we sing?" asked Daisy.

"We can sing the umari song," suggested the mischievous and daring Mona.

"No," said Keamy, very worried, "that's ngulu. Not allowed to sing umari songs."

"Who's going to see us dancing and singing here?" said Mona. "We're a long way from the station, no one will see us."

She was right, the others agreed that a little song and dance out in the bush away from the old people sounded like fun. It was like partaking of and sharing some forbidden fruit. Performing a forbidden ritual sounded like getting involved in a secret adventure.

They moved to a more secluded place, one that was surrounded by large boulders and kurrara, tangled undergrowth and prickly spinifex.

"Dinah, you go first," said the ringleader Mona. "The rest will join in and numbi (perform a woman's dance)." They sat on the boulders, while the singer stood near the hill and sang the umari song. The girls enjoyed their performance of the numbi, which was part of the marriage ceremony.

It was Mona's turn to sing when she noticed what looked like the crown of a stockman's hat moving slowly behind the kurrara bushes. Alarmed, she warned the others in a whispered voice, "You fullas, we better get up and go home."

"Why?" asked her sisters who were obviously enjoying themselves.

"There's a man going along behind the bush," she replied.

"Might be a stranger," said Dinah, hoping it was true.

But when the man appeared in the clearing, they became extremely frightened. This man was no stranger, he was Balga Burungu, Mona's brother.

"You lot a mongrel kids, what you think you doing?" he yelled angrily.

"That's a ngulu dance you were doing, and you girls know that it's ngulu," he reminded them angrily. "You mongrel lot a bastards," he said again, as he picked up a big stick and hit them hard on the legs and buttocks, swearing and becoming more furious as he delivered each stroke. This ceremonial dance is performed exclusively at ngulu time, and is a very secret dance.

Balga chased the girls all the way back to the station. They ran as fast as they could, crying out in pain as they went.

Fortunately for them the way home was downhill so they arrived home quickly. Doris's four aunts sought the safety of their respective camps, but Balga ordered them to meet him with their families at his camp.

When everyone was assembled there he explained the

reason for the meeting. He couldn't understand what possessed the girls to do such a thing. Mona was singled out by her brother who labelled her the ringleader, so naturally she received the brunt of his anger.

"Why were you singing and dancing ngulu business?" he asked, his voice filled with disappointment and disbelief.

"We went searching for mata," she told her brother, "and when we couldn't find any we look for something else to do."

"So you all wanted to numbi" The tearful four nodded.

"But why? You all know that is ngulu, that this is a very serious offence."

"I don't know what made us do it," Mona began to cry when she realised what she and her sisters had done.

"We pick it up in Jigalong, ngulu time."

"You girls want to learn to numbi, do that marriage dance properly … well, you all can go the next meeting and learn," Balga said seriously.

"No brother," they chorused, then they all pleaded and cried louder.

"We don't want to learn how to numbi properly. We don't want to get married. We had enough," said the ringleader, Mona.

"Alright," said Balga. "You can start by sitting down quietly," he told his sister, "and look after your mother Bambaru."

Mona agreed. Balga's sore and sorry little sister decided that from that day onwards all childish pranks and games must end, that she and all her sisters must behave or they would all end up being some old man's second wife. Then they would have the right to sing at the umari ceremonies.

That incident taught all four a lesson they would never forget, and that was that each one of them was responsible for her own actions, and must be prepared to accept the consequences for those actions. The girls decided that there were enough other activities to occupy them and their pesky niece.

* * *

Some of the most enjoyable times were when the seasonal changes came around. Everybody looked forward to the tropical rains in the summer months when the rain would come down in torrents. There was water everywhere, no one could enter or leave the station. The creeks and rivers filled and spilled over the banks. The station community rejoiced when there was an exceptionally good rainfall during the winter months, the prospect of a bountiful harvest of bush fruits and vegetables was anticipated. So when the warm spring weather arrived Doris accompanied her young aunts, foraging for bush tucker and searching for bush honey in native bee hives.

The native bees are much smaller than the larger commonly known European variety that produces the honey bought in shops and at road-side stalls. The native honey bees are small like house flies and have no sting. This made robbing bee hives easy. Doris had her own special billy that she filled with sweet honeycomb that she took back to the camp and shared with her grandmother. The honey was thick and dark like treacle.

* * *

The Dunnets introduced a policy that every worker regardless of age must learn to ride a horse. There was a quiet old horse reserved for this very purpose, a black station horse named "Blackie".

One day there was not one rider but four young teenagers and one little toddler, the four in this case were aunties Mona, Dinah, Chicky Burungu and Dolly Burungu, and Doris who sat proudly in the middle. As they passed the camps Molly yelled at them, "There's too many kids on that horse, you gunna kill him." The girls took no notice but rode on, waving to everyone in sight around the station.

A month or two later Molly returned to her camp from her work at the station homestead, carrying Doris on her back, she found all the girls crying. "What's the matter?" she asked, "Who passed away?" expecting bad news from outside the station.

"That old yowada, he's dead, he pass away," replied Dinah and all the girls cried even louder.

"Oh shut up, you stupid girls," ordered Molly. "You don't cry for a yowada, only for Mardu and wudgebulla." The girls weren't listening, they continued to cry.

"We want to have a funeral for old yowada," Dinah Mil-lungga told her sister.

"No, you don't have funerals for yowadas, only for people," said Molly who was becoming rather annoyed. "Where is the old yowada now?" she asked.

"Up that way, near the windmill," replied Mona wiping her eyes on the sleeve of her blouse. Doris, who had been standing quietly beside her mother, recalled her mother's warning about over-burdening that old yowada. She felt that she had a part in causing its death. But she had to be sure.

Molly carried her worried toddler to the place where the

dead horse's legs were being tied with thick rope ready to be dragged away to be buried. Doris had to check herself, she went straight for the horse's stomach and felt it, then touched its back. She was so relieved.

"His dguni is alright, not broken," she told her mother. "We never make him die."

*   *   *

Molly was still suckling two-year-old Doris on her breast until one day, while she was sitting in the shade house listening to local gossip from her fellow workers, Mary Dunnet caught her.

"That is disgusting, you stop that right now," Mrs Dunnet ordered. "She is much too big for that." The Missus didn't understand that in the Mardu community there was no time limit when breastfeeding should be discontinued. She gave Molly some tins of Nestles' condensed milk from the station store and told her how to mix it with water for Doris.

Molly took the tins back to the camp where holes were punched on opposite sides, enabling the toddler to suck the thick sweet milk. When she had enough she passed it on to her grandmother, Bambaru, then shared it with her parents. When everyone had a taste, her father took the lid off with a sharp knife, then Molly mixed it with water and gave it to her daughter to drink, like the Missus ordered.

The rest of the tins of Nestles' milk were consumed in the same way. But it didn't stop Doris from attaching herself to her mother's breast when she felt the need for comfort. Eventually Molly, under instruction from the Missus, resorted to a drastic measure and that was to rub hot mustard on her nipples the next time Doris put her hand down her bosom. And that was most effective indeed. Doris never suckled on her mother's breast again.

CHAPTER 5

Return to Moore River

Two years after Doris' dramatic birth another daughter was born to Molly, who was staying at the Jigalong Depot. Her name was Anna and she was totally the opposite of Doris. This infant was carried full term and was a beautiful, plump healthy baby. Molly loved and cared very much for this baby.

Early in September 1940, when Anna was eight months old, Molly's recurring health problem surfaced once again.

"This half-caste girl about whom there has been a lot of correspondence previously is the mother of two children and is suffering from appendicitis," reported Dr Davis. He advised Molly would have to have her appendix removed and that it would be advisable to act as soon as possible. He recommended that both Molly and her two children be removed from Balfour Downs. "She has had several attacks which have passed off." But he warned the new Commissioner for Native Affairs, Mr F. Bray, that "the next might not."

While this correspondence was being sent to and fro Molly and her family were enjoying the hot weather foraging for bush foods. Bambaru and her granddaughter delighted in each other's company and communicated in Gududjara, much to Molly's disgust — because she couldn't understand them. She preferred that they spoke Mardudjara, which was a combination of Gududjara and Mandildjara. Doris, Bambaru's first grandchild, was one of the most precious gifts that she could wish for.

Then, one fateful day, came a message over the pedal set (radio telephone) that was to rob her of that irreplaceable gift. It was from the Commissioner for Native Affairs to Bill Dunnet and it notified him that Molly and her children would be travelling with Bill Campbell by overland mail. For a fare of five pounds, paid by the Government, the woman and her little girls would be picked up at Balfour Downs Station. Molly's "black husband", so called, was to be left at the station.

Bill Dunnet replied, "We are making arrangements for them to leave here on Friday 29th of September, arriving in Meekatharra. From there Molly and her daughters will board the connecting train to Perth arriving the same night."

Molly was not told about the Department's plans to transport her to Meekatharra until the mail truck arrived on the morning to collect her and her children.

None of the family came to see them off, instead they all sat in their camps with their heads bowed in grief, weeping at the removal of Molly and her children for their long journey south. Having his wife and two daughters taken from him at the same time was too much for Toby to bear. Beside him, wailing louder than the rest, was Bambaru, whose bright red blood poured from a self-inflicted wound on her head, which was her people's traditional way of expressing deep mourning for the loss of loved ones.

Doris watched them from the back of the mail truck, her little heart was breaking. She watched until the truck turned the corner and her view was cut off. Then a veil of thick mist like a cloud of red dust fell between them, blocking out memories of her father, her beloved grandmother and all the other relatives left behind at Balfour Downs Station.

Bambaru Banaka wept and sobbed into the night, refusing to eat any food. At first light the loud wailing began again. The boss, Bill Dunnet, was aroused from his sleep, he glanced at his bedside clock, rolled over and went back to sleep.

The next morning Bambaru and Toby left the station to make a sorry camp at Ten-Mile Windmill where they made a shelter and sat down to grieve in the traditional way when a family member passes away.

Twelve months later the old woman passed away. She had mourned with her son for the loss of his family but she especially grieved for her granddaughter, Nugi Garimara, the little one who became her eyes and her companion. She missed the little arms around her neck and the child's dusty kisses on her cheek. No one could replace the child who shared her world, who had loved and cared for her and had tried to protect an old blind woman in her own small way.

* * *

Molly was brought down from Balfour Downs Station by the Department of Native Affairs to have her appendix removed at the Royal Perth Hospital. But the Department also had other plans. They would take her two children away from her as well. Special interest was focused on baby Anna who, according to the Department's classifications, was a quadroon, or three-quarters white. However, the immediate attention was on Molly herself.

"I want you to take good care of Molly," ordered the Commissioner of Native Affairs in a letter to the Superintendent of Moore River Settlement in October 1940. The Commissioner's letter explained that Molly had been removed to the settlement from Jigalong in 1931 but she absconded and got back to Jigalong. He warned that she would be likely to attempt to get away again, taking her children with her. These strict instructions were stressed because Molly had received notoriety when she and her two cousin-sisters had escaped from Moore River as teenagers in 1931 and caused the Department a lot of undesirable publicity in a search that incurred heavy expenditure. She became celebrated as the Aboriginal girl who walked 1,600 kilometres home, following the rabbit-proof fence. The Commissioner had no doubt that she might run away again, this time with her two girls. "Therefore it is essential that she should be watched as closely as possible." It was obvious that he was concerned about the negative publicity and the unwanted extra expenses. "For this reason I am most anxious that she should not abscond again."

Molly was the only Aboriginal woman about whom the Commissioner of Native Affairs expressed explicit instructions to Superintendent Paget to watch closely. But when twelve months passed by without an incident Mr Paget allowed himself to be duped into believing that Molly had settled into institutional life with no intention of escaping.

But Molly was biding her time, so when the right opportunity presented itself she grasped it with both hands.

* * *

Nearly a month after her operation Molly was reunited with her daughters at Moore River. Because Anna was still breast-feeding she was able to stay with Molly in the dormitory for the working girls. Doris, being older, was in the separate kindergarten section.

Every afternoon, after she finished her work in the settle-ment kitchen, Molly would visit Doris. She and Anna would sit outside the high steel interlock fence that surrounded the nursery and Molly would pass to Doris little treats from the kitchen.

It was almost one year later that Molly received news from Jigalong that her kinship sister Cuttapinga had died and she became very anxious that she may not be able to fulfil her obligations to Cuttapinga's son Robin. Under the kinship laws the eldest sister becomes responsible for raising the child or children of a deceased mother.

Molly approached Mr Paget and expressed her concerns for the boy's welfare. She had taken charge of Robin a short time before she left the station. The Dunnets were contacted by mail informing them that "Molly desires to have this child brought down to the Settlement".

The Deputy Commissioner of Native Affairs became in-volved at this stage; he requested more information from the Dunnets "in respect as to the name of the parents and whether Molly did have anything to do with the rearing of the child". But, most importantly, "whether the child is a half-caste or a full-blood native. Any information which you are able to supply will be appreciated."

A prompt reply was received stating that "there was no child at the station who was either fostered or cared for by Molly". Unfortunately the Dunnets and the Department were unaware of the kinship laws. The Dunnets were not aware that Molly at one stage was caring for Robin until another aunt came and took him away with her as soon as she heard that Molly was being taken to Perth for her operation. Molly had promised to come straight back.

The Department's rejection of her simple request caused distress and misery. For days Molly agonised over that problem. Then one day, what the Department had dreaded actually happened. On 4 October 1941, ten years after her notorious first escape, Molly once again absconded from Moore River. Unable to carry both her children, Molly took her baby daughter Anna with her, knowing Doris would be cared for by her aunt, Gracie Fields. Gracie had escaped with Molly on that fateful night in 1931, but had been recaptured at Wiluna and returned to Moore River.

Molly had been planning her escape since her request to bring Robin to Moore River was refused. She had promised faithfully that she would return to look after him. There was no one to take care of him now that Cuttapinga had died. Molly had already taken care of Robin on Balfour Downs while his mother was in the Loch Native Hospital. At that time Molly was breastfeeding both her daughter Doris and Robin at the same time. This created a close bond between them. She was very concerned that she could not fulfill her obligation to the boy and his family.

When the alarm went up that Molly Craig had absconded from Moore River the Commissioner knew that his department and the police were up against an older, wiser opponent who — this time carrying her baby daughter — would be even more cunning in her determination to succeed. Molly took the route familiar to her, following the rabbit-proof fence. She was born and raised along that fence, that's where she learned the survival skills to outsmart A.O. Neville in 1931. This time, ten years older and with the advantage of spring weather and the plentiful bush food and water it provided, Molly felt she had a reasonable chance of making it home to freedom once again. She chose a good time to run.

Eighteen-month-old Anna was still being breastfed when Molly made her escape, so this time there was only one mouth to feed. Working in the kitchen at Moore River gave her the opportunity to help herself to food and supplies, such as matches and a knife. The day she took off she gave her unsuspecting daughter Doris a loaf of bread to take down to an old lady in the camp. Molly was organising her escape, carefully concealing the little store of food and supplies she was building up.

Her plan was a desperate one, filled with risk, but her baby's safety was paramount. She avoided travelling in the midday heat, and listened out for surveillance aeroplanes and for the sound of the trackers' horses. Molly Craig had won their respect in the past for one of the most successful overland treks in Australian history, and certainly within their memory.

Molly knew the wheatbelt area and the farms where it

would be safe to try for handouts. This time, as a young mother with a babe in arms, it would have been hard for those on the stations to refuse requests for food. And this time she was not a girl, wearing the settlement uniform that was familiar to everyone in the countryside. Molly had her own clothing, station-made and brought down from Balfour Downs, and baby Anna was wearing an outfit that Mary Dunnet had made for her and recently sent down to Moore River.

Another reason this journey was different was that Molly did not have the pressure of Neville's obsessive determination; he had retired the previous year. As an adult Molly was not the target of the Department's search — it was young Anna. It was doubtful a search would have been made for Molly on her own. The Department's settlement practices were being wound down with the change in its policies from protectionism to assimilation.

Nearly half-way home, at Meekatharra, Molly came across a maintenance worker on the rabbit-proof fence who recognised her and gave her a lift, all the way home to Jigalong Depot.

* * *

The Commissioner of Native Affairs assumed that she would return directly to Balfour Downs Station, so a letter was dispatched in great speed. "Would you be good enough to advise me whether Molly and her child Anna have arrived at your station." His main interest was in the baby. "The little girl Anna is too white to remain in the native environment. She will have to be brought back to Moore River," he wrote.

"The girl is a quadroon and she is destined for Sister Kates, a quarter-caste home at Queens Park."

The Commissioner wanted to admit Anna as soon as there was a vacancy. He was sure that Molly was heading straight for Balfour Downs. If she did arrive at the station she would be permitted to stay there with her husband Toby. "However, we must secure Anna. She is too white to stay with Molly." Every pastoral station, every police station in the mid-west and the Upper Murchinson were alerted, "in regard to the half-caste Molly who absconded from the Moore River Native Settlement."

In April 1942 a report from the Commissioner of Native Affairs was received by Bill Dunnet at Balfour Downs advising him that all efforts to trace Molly and the child had been unsuccessful. The following month a report from Dunnet to the Commissioner's office informed him that the mother and daughter had returned some time ago to Jigalong.

Bill Dunnet volunteered to send Molly's husband Toby, who was still employed by him and had been since he was a teenager, to go and bring her to the station. Bill was annoyed that Molly may have been employed by neighbouring pastoralists. She was trained on Balfour Downs and was therefore a valuable employee. He wasn't sure whether it was Jack Matthews of Talawana, east of Balfour Downs, or Joe Criddle of Walgun Station in the south.

"I will have to fight the matter out with them," he told the Commissioner, who was very relieved when he received the news of Molly's return.

Then a most welcome report was received from Constable D.M. McMahon of the Nullagine Police Station dated July

1942 stating that "Molly Craig and her husband Toby are at Balfour Downs Station and are likely to be remaining there, at least for the time being."

As predicted Molly and her child remained at the station, right up until July the following year. Then a very concerned station owner, Bill Dunnet, reported to Constable McMahon the presence on his station of granuloma, a contagious eye disease that causes inflammation and a sand-like sensation on the inner surface of the lids. He was of the opinion that it was brought in by the newly arrived Mardus from the desert.

The policeman told the Commissioner that "there were a number of them around Balfour. The station had been free from this disease prior to the bush natives coming in and infecting others."

Molly, her baby daughter Anna and five others were admitted to the Native Hospital in Port Hedland. Matron Lund immediately sought permission from the Commissioner to employ Molly as a kitchen maid while Anna was being treated. "Thank you for considering our application to remunerate Molly while her child is an inmate at this hospital." It seems that no matter what institutions Aboriginal people were admitted to they were always referred to as an inmate, even in a hospital. The stigma continues; the older generation in Aboriginal communities today resists hospitalisation. Anna's stay was a lengthy one as far as the hospital was concerned, "the child has made a very good progress, as her infection was very serious," but, concluded Matron Lund, "she was a very bad case indeed and the progress was unusually slow."

Molly enjoyed her work at the hospital, and was able to make good friends with her co-workers and also with some of the local people — including a man named Aubrey Lockyer who fell in love with her and wanted to marry her. Molly accepted his proposal mainly because she saw this as a chance to keep her daughter Anna. But they had to apply to the Commissioner of Native Affairs for permission to marry. Not only did this Government official have the power to take children from their families, but he also had authority to control who Aboriginal and part-Aboriginal people in Western Australia could marry. This power was absolute until the 1950s.

Matron Lund certainly approved of a marriage between Molly and Aubrey Lockyer, especially as Aubrey was in employment and willing to keep and care for Anna.

The Matron liked both of them and Aubrey appeared to be an industrious type of man, she wrote to the Commissioner. But she also wanted to know, if permission was granted for the union, would Molly be able to keep her child Anna.

The pair received support from other sources as well. The Reverend Edward Bryan, the parish priest, thought that Aubrey was a steady fellow and noted that he was always in employment. He was of the opinion that Molly wanted to "better herself" by marrying out of the camp, and encouraged the Commissioner to allow the marriage to take place.

The Commissioner would not budge, he maintained his objections to the marriage. Although Molly was a "half-caste" he thought that she was too "native in character". He also objected to the disparity in their ages — Aubrey was forty-two and Molly was about twenty-seven. The Commissioner added as an afterthought that Molly already had a tribal husband.

Instructions were issued to Matron Lund that Molly be returned to Balfour Downs Station, but the Commissioner ordered that Anna was to be detained at the hospital and sent down to Sister Kates Home as soon as possible.

Nothing seemed to be going well for Molly, first the Department's intervention and objection to her proposed marriage to Aubrey Lockyer, and now they were planning to take her baby girl away from her. She was warned by one of her fellow workers that her baby was to be sent back down south as soon as she was discharged from the hospital. Molly was determined to keep her child, she had already lost her eldest daughter Doris, and didn't want the Department to take this one.

* * *

On the night of 3 October Molly quietly left the hospital with her baby. Matron Lund immediately started asking around to find the route she would take. With the assistance of two Aboriginal trackers they were able to pick up her tracks quite soon. The Matron realised that not only was Molly tough but very cunning — she made it difficult for her pursuers to track her by travelling over hard and stony country. Matron couldn't help but admire Molly who avoided roads and windmills wherever she could.

The trackers searched all day Sunday without success. On Monday they found Molly's trail five miles north of Pippingarra. Matron Lund arranged for the hire of two horses and sent the trackers after her. She concluded that Molly was travelling through the bush in a direct line for Balfour Downs.

On 4 November 1943 Matron Lund advised the Commissioner that Molly and Anna had been apprehended. They were picked up on Lalla Rookie country at midday the day before. Matron advised that they were being carefully watched, but she was convinced that Molly would try to get away again, that she seemed determined not to lose her child.

Regardless of Molly's desperate attempts to keep her baby daughter, Anna was transported south on 2 May, 1944. Anna was taken on a state ship in the care of a stewardess and, on arrival at Fremantle, she was admitted into the Sister Kates Children's Home in Queens Park, Perth.

The Commissioner breathed a sigh of relief. In his view, the "quadroon child of Molly the half-caste" was safely committed to a Government institution where she would stay until she was sixteen.

Clarrie Dunnet wrote from Balfour Downs Station a few weeks later that "Molly is here ever since she returned from Port Hedland with her husband Toby". According to Clarrie, "They appear to be getting along quite well. But in some respects it seems as though the time spent in Hedland has not improved Molly." It is not known exactly what he meant by this, but he added that from his personal observation he believed that "she seems to be forgetting her past connections down that way".

It can be presumed that he was referring to Molly's relationship with Aubrey Lockyer. But the pain of losing her baby girl was far greater than the pain of a love affair and a proposed marriage to a man in Port Hedland. Because Molly would never forget her two daughters Doris and Anna Craig.

For Molly it took several weeks to settle back into the station routine of domestic work. But those who knew her well believed that without her children she became a melancholy figure who moved around in a dream-like manner. During the evening she would sit by the fire at her camp with her husband Toby, looking morosely towards the sunset in the west.

Who was looking after her daughters, she wondered. She was comforted with the knowledge that they had older cousins and aunts to hold and cuddle them, relations who had also been removed from their families in the East Pilbara and Upper Murchison regions.

Those weeks were the most distressful for her, especially at night when her breasts were filled with milk and there was no child to suckle. The pain in her breasts was made worse by the pain in her heart. The indescribable pain of a mother in torment and grieving for her lost children. It was an ache that appeared every time she thought of them. Only time could heal that suffering, but meanwhile nothing could soothe this mother's aching heart.

The Government said that Doris and Anna were taken away to go to school down south. But that didn't make it any easier for Molly. How was a mother to cope with the absence of the sounds of her daughters? The Government, the boss and all those other people who told her that it was best for her children, how did they know how she and her man felt? The emptiness and despair, and how much she missed their warm little bodies near their mother's breast. No, they would

never know. Sometimes Molly wished she could die. But then
hope surged through her. One day she would see them again.
She would never give up hope.

One ray of hope came in May 1947 in the form of the
Aborigines Rescue Mission. This rescue mission was estab-
lished in the remote, isolated location that was formerly the
Jigalong Depot.

The Jigalong site was offered to the Apostolic Church of
Australia, a small Protestant religious sect who had been
negotiating with the government for four years to establish
a mission in the Western Desert region. The government
decided that it was time to abolish the protection policy and
legislate a new policy — the assimilation policy. The settlements were closing down, becoming obsolete, and Christian
missions were being established throughout the state under
various denominations.

Hope flared up once again for Molly. The main aim of the
missionaries was to save the souls of the desert Aborigines
whom they considered to be wanderers in the darkness who
practised sinful activities such as adultery, fornication and
devil worship. The same system of dispensing medicines,
treatment, food, rations, blankets and clothing was still in
place but now under a different administrator.

The missionaries didn't realise that they had a captive
audience who didn't understand biblical language let alone
basic English. All the school-age children were placed in
dormitories. And when Molly heard about that she saw a way
that she could have her daughters back near her. During the
summer break in 1947 she approached the Reverend Turn-

bull and discussed an idea that would have her children transferred to the Jigalong Mission.

Subsequently, Reverend Turnbull wrote to Mr McBeath, the assistant Commissioner of Native Affairs, telling him of Molly's request and assuring him that the Mission was quite willing to take over the care of both of her children if the Commissioner decided to send them there.

A month later the long-awaited reply arrived. The Commissioner's answer was detailed and to the point. "As Anna is a quarter-caste I would not be prepared to grant approval for her transfer to Jigalong Mission," he wrote, "as she is now being trained to take her place in the community as a white person, and this would not be possible of accomplishment at Jigalong. Such a decision is the only one possible in such a case, and in fairness to the child itself, as native association to the slightest degree would mitigate against the success of such a fair-coloured child."

He would be prepared to allow Doris to return to Jigalong Mission, but "before anything definite is decided, I would like you to give the matter your earnest consideration, it is doubtful that such a child has any future under such an arrangement. It must be remembered that this little girl has now been at Moore River for the past seven years and has possibly little or no memories of her parents."

So once again Molly's hope of seeing her children was utterly shattered. Sad and dejected, she and Toby returned to work at the station without any hope — just dreams of their stolen children.

CHAPTER 6

Incarceration and Alienation

Doris was three years old and her baby sister Anna was almost ten months old when they arrived at the Moore River Native Settlement on that beautiful spring day in 1940.

On their arrival the girls were taken to the kindergarten by Lorna Day who had escorted them to the Settlement. As they waited for someone to answer the door Doris stood behind Lorna, her little fingers gripping the hem of Lorna's dress tightly, and pleading in Mardudjara "Auntie, don't leave us here, take us to Mummy". The door was opened by a stern-looking woman. Doris took an instant dislike to her.

"I'm Nurse Hannah, come in," she said.

The hard-faced gaunt-looking woman stepped aside to let them in. Doris's eyes began searching for her sick mother. She appealed in language for Lorna to find her. But Lorna could not understand her, she had never learned her traditional language. One of the working girls took baby Anna from Lorna's arms while another prised the frightened Doris's fingers from her dress. The girls carried the new arrivals into the dining room where the carers were preparing the children's lunch.

"Auntie, wait for me, don't leave me here," screamed the panic-stricken child as she was carried kicking and screaming and shoved into the arms of a carer named Gracie.

"See if you can settle this wild one," said Kathy, one of the older girls.

"What's her name?" Gracie wanted to know.

"Lorna Day said the big one's name is Doris and the baby is Anna."

"Where did they come from?"

"From a station up north somewhere," replied Kathy.

"Did she mention the name?" Gracie thought to herself, there was something familiar about this little girl. "What's their mother's name?"

"Their mother is Molly Craig and they're from Balfour Downs Station up Meekatharra way." Tears filled Gracie's eyes and spilled down her cheeks.

"What's wrong?" her co-worker asked.

"These two little ones are my cousin's daughters," Gracie told them as she wiped her eyes. By now Doris had calmed down and was eyeing the four young women warily.

"Nurse Hannah says their mother is in the Royal Perth Hospital," said Rita, "but she will be coming here when she is better."

Gracie took her niece out on to the verandah.

"See, there's lots of other boys and girls to play with," she told Doris. But the child wasn't interested, she preferred to stay near her aunt Gracie.

Gracie had become overwhelmed with melancholy as

memories of the event that took place almost ten years before returned to her. She could still remember how Doris and Anna's mother Molly, herself and another cousin-sister escaped from this very place. It was the most frightening experience of her life. She was the unlucky one, the one who was captured in Wiluna and brought back to Moore River. The other two walked all the way back home to Jigalong, 1,600 kilometres. She longed for her mother Yowie and all her other relations at Jigalong and Walgun Station.

She quietly sat with her arm around her little niece and smiled to herself as she thought of the way of life on a cattle station in the East Pilbara that she and these little ones had left behind. She brightened up when she thought of meeting up with her cousin-sister again, they had a lot of catching up to do.

"Come on Doris, let's go and meet the rest of the kids," her aunt said as she picked her up off the veranda and walked towards the playground where the kindergarten children were involved in all sorts of imaginative games.

Doris was introduced to the rest of the children. They stopped playing to give a quick glance then continued their games. "And that big girl with the long black hair is Lizzie Ray." Lizzie, like Rita Sambo, came from the Esperance–Norseman region.

"You stop here and play with the others," said Gracie. "I have to go back in the kitchen and do some work."

"Don't leave me here, take me with you," cried Doris, her two small arms wrapped around Gracie's leg. This would be the third time today that Doris had found comfort with a stranger only to be passed on to someone else.

Doris clung on firmly. Gracie very carefully took her tiny hands, loosened their grip and told her once again, "Go and play with the others."

Then she suddenly stopped as the child spoke in a language she had not heard for many years, "Where is Bambaru, and my Mummy and Daddy?" As Gracie looked down at the small sad face it almost made her cry.

She took Doris by the hand and led her away from the group, and told her very quietly: "You must not speak language here, alright?"

Doris nodded. "I'll be back after. You go and play," promised her auntie and they returned to the group where Lizzie persuaded the timid Doris to join them. Lizzie was a pretty young woman who had a soft voice and a beautiful smile. Time passed very quickly, soon the lunch bell rang and Lizzie and all her charges went to wash their hands and faces. Then they filed into the dining room to eat a lunch of mutton stew, bread and butter, and a drink made from powdered milk. After lunch all the smaller babies including Anna were sponged over and placed in their cots for an afternoon nap while the rest amused themselves outside in the playground.

The kindergarten was a self-contained building situated between the staff quarters and the pine plantation. The children were provided with meals cooked by Gracie, and assisted by Rita, Nancy Punch, and Alice Smith, a young woman from the Kimberley region. This was part of their training for future employment as domestic help to white families who could hire them for the total sum of fifteen shillings (about $1.50) per week. Of this they were given seven shillings and sixpence (75¢) pocket money, the rest was sent back to the Department of Native Affairs to deposit in a bank account for them.

The nursery was a large overcrowded rectangular room filled with white painted iron cots so close together that the children could touch each other through the bars. There were bars on the windows — the few mothers at the settlement were forbidden to enter the nursery to nurse and cuddle their babies and toddlers.

Eventually Doris gained enough courage to leave her auntie Gracie's side for longer periods each day. It was due to the efforts of two little boys named Tony and Andrew Onslow, whose surname was derived from the town from which they came, the same way many in the settlement community were identified. Doris's auntie was Grace Jigalong, it didn't matter that she was known by her family as Gracie Fields. Doris liked her new friends because they let her be the leader. So she decided their activities and games.

But the most painful adjustment that Doris had to make was sleeping by herself in the overcrowded nursery in a cot jammed between others. The first two weeks were the worst, there was no Mum, Dad or Bambaru to keep her safe and comfort her.

Routinely a child would wake up in the early hours of the morning soaking wet, cold and anxious for the comforting body of the mother who once was always there beside them. Like Doris, the most recent arrivals would wake and feel around the confines of the cot only to discover no one there, and when their tiny fingers jarred against the cold steel rods the child would cry out, "Mummy, Mummy". Then they would pause for a couple of seconds, listening for a response to their summons for love and comfort. When there was no response, they would repeat the call, "Mummy, Mummy".

At last, footsteps on the floorboards, not bare-footed ones but heavy slippered steps. That didn't matter — at least someone was answering their cry. It would be Nurse Hannah, her shadow looming on the wall of the nursery and magnified by the glow of her hurricane lamp. The whimpering would stop as she approached the cots. The light of the lamp would shine on the babies' faces as they looked up and saw the gaunt face of the nurse. Instead of a comforting hug the toddler would receive a smack on the bottom and be told roughly, "Go back to sleep at once, and stop crying." The piteous sobbing would go on until the child, emotionally drained, drifted off to sleep.

* * *

In the lonely nights and the dark despair
I called your name your voice to hear
But the loneliness and silence I learned to bear.
From the song "The Rhythm of Love"

Every new arrival would trigger off a flood of memories, like the day a little girl named Gladys who, with her sister Evelyn and four brothers, arrived from Cue, a town in the Upper Murchison. It was a busy place with children arriving at varying intervals. Some came from places hundreds of miles away to settle in their newly appointed home — this cold motherless building where the only comfort was daily contact with young Aboriginal women who were the unpaid trainee domestic staff working as cooks, childcare nurses and laundresses.

Gladys was the most recent addition to the kindergarten and, being the youngest of six, always had others around her and wasn't timid like Doris. Her aunt Rene Robinson lived down at the camps among the settlement employees, married families who had children in the compound. Rene brought her to the kindergarten that morning and handed her over to Nurse Hannah. Gladys played happily with Doris and the other children. In the late afternoon she became worried, there was no sign of her auntie Rene whom she expected to come and take her home to her cottage down at the camps. Auntie Rene never came. Gladys became another casualty of the Government's protection policy. That evening she allowed herself to be bathed and dressed in a nightie like Doris and the rest of the girls but protested loudly when she was lifted into her cot and told to go to sleep

"I don't want to stay here," she made it clear to Lizzie and Rita.

"Shush," whispered Lizzie, "Nurse Hannah will come and smack you." As their carers left the nursery Gladys took up her protest but this time with more urgency. "Come on you fullas, take me home now," she pleaded. There was no reply. She cried out again; still there was no response. So she gave up. All around her the other children slept, and soon Gladys joined them.

Some time later she awakened and, like other new arrivals, her little fingers reached out to touch a warm body but found instead the cold bars of her cot prison.

"Auntie Rene! Come and get me and take me away from this place," she cried. This time others were roused and began to cry too, each hoping that their mother would miraculously appear and take them home.

They heard the slippered footsteps and saw the glow of the lamp, and, instantly, there was silence except for the lone voice of little Gladys calling for her auntie Rene. Nurse Hannah stood outside the door and listened. Once she located the culprit she marched up to the toddler's cot, smacked her soundly, tossed her roughly down in the cot and ordered, "Be quiet and go back to sleep, you naughty girl." Like all the other occupants of all the white iron cots in the nursery, Gladys learned to settle down and accept her fate, each child having gone through the same emotional experience and survived.

Those children who had been awakened by the plaintive cries of another motherless child shut their eyes tightly and pretended to be asleep. When the crying ceased they snuggled down under the blankets and dozed back off to sleep. As the numbers of children increased, nights like this one became more frequent.

Although the mothers and other relatives were forbidden to enter the kindergarten, they had regular contact along the boundary fence. Doris and Anna had to wait for almost one month before their mother Molly was brought from the Royal Perth Hospital and was able to see them again. Like many of the more fortunate mothers, Molly, who worked in the settlement kitchen, had daily contact with her daughters in the secluded spot under the pine trees near the kindergarten. There, women were permitted to talk to their children but physical contact was not allowed. Many mothers disregarded that instruction by those in authority and, with the cooperation of the working girls, were able to nurse and cuddle their children.

The highlight of these visits were the treats of special foods such as hot damper dripping with butter, warm sweet milky tea and sometimes fruit and lollies. Because Anna was still breastfed she was allowed to live with her mother in the working girls' dormitory. While Molly was working in the kitchen another nursing mother took care of her baby. At the settlement all breastfeeding mothers were on stand-by, ready to step in as a substitute mum and minder to any baby needing them.

Doris looked forward to the daily visits from her mother and baby sister. She knew what time to sit down and wait, she was told to watch for a certain time of the day when the sun reached a special place in the sky. Every day at the same time she had the joy of meeting with her mother and baby sister Anna. She shared the special treats her mother would bring with her playmates Tony and Andrew.

These meetings under the pine trees went on for weeks and months. A whole year passed, then one day Molly and Anna didn't show up. Doris waited and waited until late afternoon when Kathy came to collect her.

"Come on Doris, it's nearly tea time," Kathy told her as she reached for the toddler's small hand and held it firmly in her own.

"Your mother and little sister might come tomorrow," Kathy said as they walked to the kindergarten. When her two friends saw her sad face they asked Doris, "What's the matter?"

"My mother never came today," she answered, her lip quivering as the tears began to fall.

"Don't cry Doris, have a bath and some tea and tomorrow you'll see your mother and Anna," assured Kathy. Doris liked Kathy Ryder, a Nyoongah girl who was a well-built, fair young woman with the right personality for a childcare nurse.

So every day for a whole week Doris waited at her special place for two special individuals to show up. They never appeared. She stood by that place and waited each day until all memories of them faded away. What Doris didn't know was that Molly had absconded on that clear moonlit night in October 1941 while Doris was sleeping behind the barred windows of the kindergarten nursery. There was no time for tearful farewells, her mother and sister had slipped away in the night leaving Doris in the care of her aunt Gracie.

* * *

CHAPTER 7

Hardship and Friendship

O F THE MANY CHILDREN she could form friendships with, Doris was drawn to an unlikely pair, the two Onslow brothers, Andrew and Tony who were brought to Moore River from a small town in the Pilbara with their mother Tiny and their auntie Gladys. Doris became the leader and the instigator of their childhood exploits.

One day the three friends were caught digging up and eating dry, withered carrots in a disused garden plot. They were smacked and told, "That stuff's rubbish!" The trio hung their heads in shame as the other children giggled. It was most embarrassing. The three used to eat bush foods similar to the root vegetables found in the gardens. Although the toddlers were not speaking their language and the memories of the families left behind were fading, they still remembered the smell and taste of bush foods. The shriveled, dried carrots reminded the trio of the mata that grew throughout the Pilbara region.

After that incident Doris, Andrew and Tony decided to sit quietly on the front lawn behind the steel-roped barrier and watch the adults as they passed up and down the gravel road. Then suddenly — before any of the working girls could stop her — Doris leaped up, bounded across the lawn and dived under the fence. She ran to two Mardu women and did what was the natural thing to do at the time, and that was to communicate in Mardu wangka.

"Aunties," she addressed the startled women, "where's Bambaru?" The two women stopped and stared down at the child who repeated the question in language, anxiously awaiting a reply.

"Where's Bambaru?" she asked once again.

They looked at each other and spoke in their own tongue. "What is this little one saying?" inquired the woman on the right.

"I don't know," replied her companion. "I think she might come from Marble Bar or Nullagine way."

"No, I can't pick that wangka up, poor little girl must be a long way from her country."

Doris couldn't understand why they didn't answer her. They were from the Kimberley region and had come to the settlement while their father recovered from surgery at the Royal Perth Hospital. He had fallen off his horse and broken his leg. They would return home when he was discharged.

Before Doris could repeat the question, she was roughly lifted over the fence and smacked on her bare legs. It was Nurse Hannah who caused this pain — to punish a child who dared to "talk to natives" and in "native language". Doris hadn't spoken Mardu wangka for a whole year, even when her mother visited her. The strange thing was that when she saw the Mardu women she automatically slipped into her traditional language.

"You're a very naughty girl, you must not talk blackfella language again," yelled Nurse Hannah. "You understand?" Gracie came and took her sobbing niece from the charge nurse out to the front verandah.

"Never mind, don't cry now," said Gracie, rubbing Doris's painful legs. Her two friends came and sat down near her. Andrew, his voice quivering in sympathy, said "Don't cry, Doris."

"Our Mum will come up and smack her, and make her cry, unna Gracie," added Tony. Gracie nodded in agreement. Doris was comforted by the prospect of seeing the boys' mother Tiny give their nurse a hiding. She felt much better.

"Come on, let's go and play on the seesaw," said Doris.

"Wait a minute," said her auntie, as she pulled a hankie from her bosom and wiped her niece's eyes, then kissed her on the forehead. Doris slid off her auntie Gracie's lap and went off happily with her playmates. The three friends played on the seesaw until they were called in to wash their faces and hands and get ready for lunch.

Learning not to speak their own wangka was not the only adjustment the children had to make. The settlement clothes also caused problems — especially for the girls. When there was a shortage of elastic for their bloomers, that were made on the settlement, white tape was substituted. It was no problem first thing in the morning when the childcare nurses dressed the girls and tied the bows for them. It was when the little girls had to go to the toilet — they had no idea how to tie bows and knotted the tape instead. Many accidents occurred and the messy bloomers would be tossed anywhere near the laundry. All was revealed when the girls joined in the fun and games in the playground. Soon every child in the group would know who was "being rude" by exposing their private parts. Nurse Hannah complained to Sister Eileen, the Church of England nun who administered to the spiritual needs of the settlement community, and also taught the women dressmaking. The excuse was always the same, "There's a war on. It is very difficult to get orders filled. We have to make do with what we have." Then one day there were yards and yards of elastic for dozens of bloomers. It didn't matter whether they were made from the same material that the men's and boy's pyjamas were made from, as long as they had elastic in the waist — that's all that mattered.

* * *

A few weeks later Doris, Andrew, Dolores and Tony decided to make a big cubby house of dried pine needles. It took some time to gather enough to form the walls of a cubby house where they sat and pretended to be adults. The boys became hunters and the girls were mums playing cards. They agreed that they needed more pine needles to build their walls higher. Among the pine needles Doris found some strange black peels. She sniffed them and passed them on to the boys to smell.

"What is this?" she said softly.

"I don't know," they replied.

"It smells good," said Doris beginning to chew on it, then passed it back to her playmates to try.

"I know what that is," said Delores sniffing the unpleasant-looking withered fruit peel, "that's a binana." She would know: Delores and her father Peter Prior had been brought down from Carnarvon in the Gascoyne region where there were banana plantations.

"You get big ones like that," she informed them, demonstrating with both hands, "you peel the binana, eat the inside and chuck the skin away."

"I'll chuck it away somewhere," volunteered Doris as she walked towards the heap of pine needles behind the pine trees. But she had no intention of getting rid of the banana skin, because curiosity had got the better of her. She began to chew a piece, then passed it on to Andrew and Tony. At that moment Delores turned around.

"Lizzie," she shouted to the carer, "look at Doris, Andrew and Tony, they're eating binana skins."

"You three rubbish eaters!" Lizzie said as she snatched the bits of peels from their hands. "Spit that out too," she ordered them angrily. "You want to get sick and die?"

"No, we don't want to die," said Andrew.

Rita came over from her group of children to see what the fuss was all about.

"The three rubbish eaters are at it again," said Lizzie pointing to Doris and the two brothers who sat in the pine cubby, rubbing their eyes. They were feeling humiliated, being referred to as "rubbish eaters". For the next few weeks they resisted the temptation to sample any scraps of food that looked edible.

The trio kept to themselves, inventing their own games and amusing themselves by floating off into the land of make believe. They discovered they couldn't get into trouble with imaginary beings such as giants, fairies and angels. No one smacked them or mocked them. Sometimes some of the other boys and girls joined in the games about hunting and gathering.

They had all their meals in the communal dining room. The food was terrible, for breakfast weavilly porridge, and watery stews for dinner. Sometimes there was treacle or golden syrup on their bread, sometimes dripping. No wonder the children missed their bush foods.

Then one day Doris spotted something exciting, its colour was stimulating — shiny blue wrapping paper with pretty silver stars all over it, and an aroma that was divine.

"Look, I found another one," squealed Tony. He sniffed at the red wrapper with silver stars. "These must have come from heaven." They called the others to come and look at the precious bits of treasure they had found.

The trio from the north-west was enlightened immediately.

"That's chocolate," said Isabel from Moora. "Someone had Easter beggs." Doris, Andrew and Tony were very disappointed. Their illusion that it fell from heaven, an angel's food, was shattered.

"It must taste loverly," said Doris wistfully.

"Yes," agreed Andrew, "I wish I had some."

"Me too," said his brother. They decided to play some other game until tea time.

One afternoon, when they were quietly playing under the branches of the pine trees Doris saw something that made her little heart beat fast with excitement. Burning through the spaces of the pine plantation a short distance away was a brightly lit fire. Before anyone could stop her, she leaped up and ran towards the fire.

"Bambaru," she called with joy, for to her the blazing fire was a symbol of home and, most of all, of the warmth of her parents' and her blind grandmother's love. It triggered special memories of the three people whom she loved and missed so much.

"Mummy, Daddy, Bambaru," she squealed with anticipation. Her friends watched in stunned silence as Doris headed for the fire. But her happiness and joy were cut short when Rita Sambo caught up with her, picked her up and took her to Nurse Hannah.

"How many times must you be told," Nurse Hannah said as she smacked Doris soundly on her bare bottom. The nurse hit harder this time, emphasising the consequences for the benefit of all the incarcerated children: "No talking to black natives and no talking native language!"

Doris was dumped on her sore bottom near her two friends who tried to comfort her.

"Don't cry, Doris," Tony patted his friend on the arm, "it's all right." The other children, curious, gathered around them asking, "what happened?" Why did Rita, their quietly spoken, favourite childcare nurse take Doris to Nurse Hannah for punishment?

"Nothing," answered the two boys.

"You been eating rubbish again?" asked Delores.

"No, we never ate any rubbish, so there," replied an angry Andrew.

"What then?" asked Cliffie.

"Nothing," answered Tony.

"Why did Nurse Hannah smack Doris?" Delores asked.

"For trying to run away to the black fullas' campfire," Tony told the children who had come to listen. "It was up there," he said, pointing to where a blazing fire was burning so brightly that it was like an enticing beacon to a former station child.

But it was what that fire represented that was important. The next morning, as soon as she was let out to play, Doris was like a moth drawn to a candle flame as she headed for the pine plantation. She stood silently, her young eyes searching for the fire and the friendly images she knew had stood around it. But sadly there was nothing but the pine trees. "I can't see anything. It was just a dream," thought Doris. There were no images or figures warming themselves around the fire. Standing inside the boundary fence sad and alone Doris understood, this was a lesson and she could pretend no longer. She decided that she had enough of smacks and being humiliated in front of the other incarcerated children, and so from that day forth she would become a child with no past. All her memories would be suppressed. This was a mutual experience for all incarcerated Aboriginal children and adults, who now have no culture, no language, no history, no people. Like the blazing fire that had burned so cheerfully, the memories flicker and then die, extinguished forever.

What Doris didn't know was that the visitors were real. They were strangers who had come down from the Kimberley with a sick family member who was transferred to the settlement to recuperate from a surgical operation at the Royal Perth Hospital. They would return to their homelands when the patient recovered. They were ordered to move and make a camp away from the kindergarten. They were informed by Nurse Hannah that the Department had instructed all staff that there was to be no contact between the children and "natives". The authorities didn't want the residents' lives interrupted by reminders of their past.

In Doris's case pain was the decision maker and the forceful persuader. Combined with daily reinforcement to forget the past, it proved effective indeed. With their mothers, grandmothers and other blood relations behind an invisible wall of silence and obscurity, all traces of their memories vanished. All the children's links to their traditional and cultural past were severed forever.

Like all children Doris could not remain maudlin for long, she and her playmates always found something to amuse themselves, so they turned to the games that other boys and girls enjoyed. There were squabbles and disputes over leadership and who controlled the activities. But everywhere the children went, they were supervised by Lizzie, Rita, Kathy and Nancy who were not mothers or grandmothers but who were Aboriginal and at least knew the young children's world. On most days Doris and the Onslow boys initiated the activities, and the others participated.

One morning the three friends woke up to find that the hot summer weather was over, and cool, crisp autumn had descended on the unsuspecting children at the kindergarten. The leaves of the plane trees near the stone wall, built to protect the staff from potential intruders, were turning all shades from yellow to brown.

The boys and girls enjoyed playing with the damp sand,

making sand castles and all sorts of different sand sculptures. They loved digging dams and rock holes and creating long winding rivers. One day the small group of children was sitting near the stone wall that divided the kindergarten and the staff quarters, when a beautiful little robin redbreast flew onto the leafless plane tree.

"Oh, look there," exclaimed Andrew pointing to the brightly coloured bird. "That's a robin redbreast." All little eyes were focused on the beautiful bird which stood out against the bare limbs of the tree.

"How do you know it's a robin redbreast?" asked Cliffie.

"Because Kathy told us, unna Doris?" said Andrew. "And you know what else she told us," he added, feeling very proud that he knew something they did not.

"No, tell us," pleaded the others.

"Well, Kathy told us a story," said Tony, not waiting for his brother. "She said that a long time ago, a robin, like that one, tried to take the prickles off Jesus's head, and he got pricked and the prickle made him bleed," he finished rather seriously.

"Oh, poor thing," chorused the sad group. As they sat watching the lone robin, their empathy was projected onto the small bird flittering in and out of the branches. To overcome the gloom Doris began to sing a song that their carers had taught them a few weeks previously.

Little birdie on the tree, on the tree, on the tree,
Little birdie on the tree, sing a song to me.
Sing about the blossoms on the tree so tall.
Sing about the roses on the garden wall.
Little birdie on the tree, sing a song to me.

At that moment a miracle occurred: four other robins joined the first one. They darted in and out of the plane tree, then chirped loudly in unison before flying off into the pine trees. The children clapped their hands with glee, then remained seated on the ground waiting for the robins' return. But they never appeared again.

* * *

Then came the winter rains, driven by the winds from the coast to the settlement. Terrible storms occurred during the night, the terrifying winds whistled beneath the guttering, thunder crashed overhead and rumbled on. The storms often continued for hours during the night. The flashes of lightning lit the whole building, revealing for a quick second the tiny forms shivering under their cot blankets and wishing for the comforting warmth of their loving mothers. No one could imagine how terrifying it was for these tiny human beings during those stormy nights.

Cries of "Mummy, Mummy, Mummy, come here," filled the overcrowded nursery. Then would come the sounds of the slippered feet on the creaking wooden floorboards, and the glow of the hurricane lamp. All crying ceased instantly.

The rains prevented the children from playing outdoors, there was nowhere else to play but on the verandahs. So if the rain was coming from the south, the children would play on the east side and if the rain came from the north, the south verandah was the dry place. At regular intervals the childcare nurses would glance up to the skies hoping to see a break in the weather. They were getting fed up with the crying, grizzling babies and toddlers who protested against being cooped up all day on the verandah. Then, one morning, the children would awaken to discover the grey, dull rain clouds had disappeared, replaced by blue skies and fluffy white clouds.

"Lizzie, can we go outside to play?" asked Delores. The young woman checked the weather, then gave her permission. The children all made straight for the seesaw and swings. Up and down, up and down they would go, four on each side, perfectly balanced, giggling and chatting about everything and nothing. They were joined by Tommy Dawson and Gordon Willock.

"You know what," said Gordon excitedly. "Kathy said that the river is running." This annual occurrence brought the whole settlement together. The news was overheard by the two usually shy boys and it created interest and curiosity amongst Doris and her playmates.

They couldn't remember what "running river" meant, but were sure it was an event not to be missed.

"I want to go and see the river," said Delores.

"Me too," chorused the rest.

"Kathy said, when the river is flooded, everybody goes down to see it," Gordon told them.

"I want to see the flood," said Tony.

"Come on then," responded his older brother Andrew. "Let's go," he said, pushing his friend Doris towards his brother.

Six out of the group made a move to go down to the cliffs, the vantage point for viewing the river. The others became very concerned. "You'll get a hiding from Nurse Hannah," warned Lena. This was just the adventure Doris and the brothers needed after being cooped up on the verandahs for days. The trio and the three other curious youngsters chose not to heed the warning from their other playmates and headed off towards the steel-roped fence and crawled under to freedom.

The defiant children ran towards the cliffs and stood close to the edge. From high on the cliffs the view took their breath away. Doris was captivated by the scene below just as her mother Molly, then a fourteen-year-old girl, had been in 1931, ten years before.

There was water everywhere, trees and shrubs were partly submerged in the chocolate-coloured river. The children watched and listened with awe. The wonder of the sight that met their small eyes was even more fantastic than they could imagine — swirling currents, and white foam that clung to the trunks of the paperbark trees and the tall river gums.

While the sightseers were chattering excitedly about the points of interest Kathy and Lizzie stood near the sand dunes watching and pondering how to approach their charges without startling them. They were acutely aware that, if startled, their charges could fall down the steep face of the white chalk cliff.

Kathy called out calmly, "Hey, you naughty kids, you know you shouldn't be out of the yard."

"Look, Kathy, the river is running!"

"Yes, I know, I saw it", she said in a steady voice as the children started back, climbing under the fence.

"You are all very naughty kids. You could have fallen off the cliffs." They were used to being cautioned and admonished by Lizzie and Kathy who never carried out their threats to smack them — unless it was absolutely necessary. They were filled with joy and happiness at what they had just seen. Yes, the river was running so deep and wide. Their knowledge united them with the wider settlement community.

The six adventurers chatted happily as they walked beside their nurses. "Did you see this?" "Did you see that?" They had no idea of what fate awaited them. The penalty for being out of bounds and for endangering their own lives was decisive and cruel. On arrival at the kindergarten the four boys and Doris and Lena, whose mother came from Sharks Bay in the Gascoyne region, were delivered to Nurse Hannah. When they saw the expression on the nurse's face they knew their fear of her was well-founded. Doris's thin legs trembled with fear as she moved closer to her friends for protection.

"Now who is the ringleader?" Nurse Hannah bellowed.

"Not me." "Not me," answered the nervous children. She looked around and chose her first victim, the very shy boy from Yalgoo in the Upper Murchison.

"Gordon Willock," she demanded, "come here." The boy began to cry but that didn't stop Nurse Hannah as she lifted him onto the table used to change babies and toddlers. She pulled his shorts down roughly and whacked his bare bottom with the long cane. Gordon screamed for his mother to come and save him. Rita took him outside to comfort him.

Nurse Hannah looked around for her next victim, and grabbed the trembling Cliffie — his cousin Kathy had gone out to check on the other children who were playing in the playground. While sharing the playground duties, she called to the young men who were sitting outside the dining room smoking and talking. When they learned what was happen-

ing at the kindergarten, they sent a runner to the camps and
around the compound to tell them "Miss Hannah is flogging
the kindy kids."

Kathy returned to discover that her cousin Cliffie had
received the harsh punishment that had been inflicted on
Gordon and Lena. She took him outside to try to soothe his
pain. Meanwhile Doris, Tony and Andrew stood together
waiting to be led like lambs to the slaughter. Doris was the
next to receive the cane. The pain was so excruciating that
the tiny girl almost passed out. She waited in fear, tightening
her buttocks for the next blow. But fortunately it never came.

She heard scuffling behind her, then she heard Lizzie
pleading with her auntie Gracie, "Don't do it Gracie. You'll
get six months in Fremantle." Doris saw that her aunt had
snatched the cane from Nurse Hannah's hand and was about
to strike her, but the nurse dashed to the safety of her
quarters. Meanwhile a large crowd had gathered outside the
entrance of the kindergarten, concerned mothers and other
relations asking who had been flogged by Miss Hannah.

"Did she flog my daughter? My son? Is my niece alright?"
and so on.

Gracie carried her sobbing niece to the fence to display
the welt across her bottom to her relations on the other side
of the six-foot wire fence where the community was gathering. There was lots of grumbling and angry threats of what
they intended to do to this person for her treatment of their
children. Luckily, Tony and Andrew escaped the punishment
that their friends had endured.

Gracie sat down on the ground inside the kindergarten
fence and held a damp flannel on her niece's aching bottom.

She wiped Doris's face gently. Seated on either side of her were Tony and Andrew who were crying softly for their special friend. At that moment their mother Tiny and auntie Gladys approached the fence on the other side and sat down.

"Are you all right?" asked their mother. The boys nodded.

"Miss Hannah is cruel, Mummy. She flogged Doris, Lena, Cliffie and Gordon, and, and — boo, hoo," they cried louder.

"Mummy," said Andrew. "You and auntie Gladys gunna flog her?" Tiny replied by assuring them that everything would be alright. The two boys calmed down.

The people in the crowd outside were talking quietly amongst themselves. Suddenly all conversation ceased. Mr Paget, the superintendent, had arrived at the request of Nurse Hannah. She was worried about the crowd that had gathered outside the kindergarten.

"Look, Mr Paget, see what that cruel woman did to my niece?" Gracie said as she blocked his entry through the gate.

"Please everyone, leave this to me," he said quietly as he did his best to pacify the angry adults. He was very worried, he didn't want the crowd to get out of control. He was aware that there has never been a situation like this before where the "natives" had protested vocally against a white staff member.

Mr Paget had learned during his short term in office that the settlement "natives" had a high tolerance to pain. They accepted physical punishment with little or no protest. But harm a child — then it was a different matter. The "natives" would go through hell and high water for their children. He was only too aware that abuse of children was not tolerated in their society.

Mr Paget entered the kindergarten where the carers were comforting the other children who were still suffering from the wrath of the cruel, childless woman. They told him what had occurred. When the superintendent reappeared before the angry parents and relatives, he wore a serious expression. The crowd stood up and waited in silence for his response.

"Everything has been settled," he assured them. "Miss Hannah has been sacked, so please go home now. Your children will be alright."

The news of the nurse's dismissal was accepted in the same spirit that it was announced, in sincerity and the hope that their children would never be abused again. The crowd dispersed quietly except Gracie, Tiny, Gladys, and the three friends. The women talked quietly amongst themselves for a little while longer.

The news of Miss Hannah's dismissal was greeted with delight and relief. She was transported during the night to the Mogumber siding where she boarded the train to Perth. She was never heard of again.

Her replacement was a pleasant woman named Miss Marshal who was just what the motherless children needed. She was a caring person who was loved by all the kindergarten boys and girls. Under Miss Marshal's management improvements were introduced to assist the growth and development of her charges. These included daily walks in the afternoons, weather permitting. Doris, Tony and Andrew enjoyed these little excursions in the bush around the boundary fences. They were the introduction to lessons in bush craft and searching for bush or traditional foods found in the area.

But unfortunately, not all childcare nurses were responsible, caring young women. There was an incident that shocked the settlement community. A new girl was rostered at the kindergarten, her name was Mary Masters. One beautiful, spring afternoon while most of the children were playing in the gravel pit, which was 500 yards away from the kindergarten, a thin little boy named Johnny Jones was beaten up by Mary Masters and four of his so-called playmates. They used green sticks which left scratches on his face. When the group returned to the kindergarten Mary reported that Johnny had fallen down into the gravel pit.

"He never fell down, Auntie," whispered Doris to Gracie. "Mary gave him a hiding, and she made the other kids hit him too." Kathy, Rita, Gracie and Nancy felt sorry for this timid child who wouldn't harm a fly.

The story spread all over the settlement. The next day Mary Masters was admitted to hospital, badly beaten in the working girls' dormitory by persons unknown. Her behaviour was reported to Mr Leeming, the new Superintendent. He handed her over to the police at Moora, and instructed them to send her out to work after she served her time. In time Johnny recovered from his ordeal and all the scars disappeared.

* * *

Before they knew it Christmas had arrived. The kitchen and dining room were decorated with streamers of all different colours. There was an air of excitement as Christmas cheer spread.

"Father Christmas is coming soon," this message was bandied around for almost two weeks.

"When is Father Christmas coming?" the children won-

dered. But many children like Doris and the Onslow brothers had never seen him so they were looking forward to
meeting a special man named Father Christmas. As usual
Doris woke at dawn, to discover something hanging from the
rail at the end of her cot.

"Andrew, Tony," she called out excitedly, "wake up, it's
Christmas time." Soon all the sleepy little forms were waking
and they stood up in their cots, some removing their soaking
night gowns, then focusing their eyes on the object hanging
at the end of their cots.

What was it? No one knew. Doris lifted the thing off the
steel rod and sat down in the cot to examine it closely. It was
a khaki military sock which, for the Aboriginal children on
the settlement, served as a Christmas stocking. It was filled
with one red apple, one green apple, an orange, and two
milk arrowroot biscuits decorated with blue icing sugar for
the boys and pink for the girls, and sprinkled with hundreds
and thousands. In the bottom of the sock were some boiled
lollies of different colours, liberally covered with sugar. This
certainly was Christmas. Soon all the children in the nursery
— except the babies — were sitting in their cots, some still
in their soaking-wet night clothes, munching or crunching
on some treat they had found in their Christmas stocking.
The children had difficulty trying to find enough room for
their normal breakfast of porridge, bread and butter with
golden syrup and a cup of milk.

Christmas dinner was wonderful. There was roast mutton
and all the trimmings, followed by jelly and custard, cup
cakes, lollies, and homemade cordial. There were no presents but all the children agreed that Christmas Day — Jesus's

birthday — was a wonderful day for them, and for the staff who made it special.

CHAPTER 8

The Big School

THE YEARS ROLLED ON BY, soon it was time for Doris, Tony and Andrew to join their friends at the "big" school. For the past year they had attended the infants school that was attached to the kindergarten.

"That means that all the boys and girls who were in Miss Chapman's class last year will be going to the 'big' school," Miss Marshal informed them.

"We'll be going down to the compound with all the big kids," said Andrew excitedly. They were looking forward to seeing all the older boys and girls. But they didn't notice that Doris had reverted to her timid self. Attending the "big" school with all the big kids staring at her sounded frightening.

"I want to stay here," she said quietly. "I want to stay with my auntie Gracie."

"But Doris, you'll see your auntie Gracie when we go to the compound," Andrew reminded his anxious friend. Doris needed her auntie right now. "Auntie," she called out as she raced off to the kitchen to find her. But she wasn't there, she had gone. Gone where?

"Kathy, where's Gracie?" asked Andrew.

"She's gone out to work."

"But where's she gone?"

"I don't know where, but Mr Leeming found her a job somewhere," Kathy told them. She saw that Doris's eyes were brimming with tears. "Don't cry, Doris, your auntie is coming back to see you," said Kathy. But Doris didn't believe her. Everybody said that to her but they never kept their promise.

They started at the big school on that cold, grey Monday morning. The small group of eight children walked beside their childcare nurses, Lizzie, Kathy and Rita, to the big school in the top end of the compound. Miss Marshal and the kitchen staff, Nancy and Alice, who had replaced Gracie, waved to them as they made their way to school, a daunting experience for any child, but particularly for Doris whose only carers had been the kindergarten staff. Luckily it wasn't raining. Doris felt special in her navy blue woolen frock with a Peter Pan collar as she walked between her two playmates Andrew and Tony Onslow. They were taken and introduced to their new teacher Mrs Brenchley, a stocky Yorkshire woman who proved to be a very skilled teacher and who obviously enjoyed teaching Aboriginal children. The bell rang and they were instructed to stand in line in front of the whole school.

"Good morning, boys and girls," said a rather large lady.

"Good morning, Miss Holland," responded the children in unison.

"Ah," she said, "there are some new boys and girls here today. Welcome to you all," she added with enthusiasm.

Doris fidgeted nervously, not daring to look up at the two teachers standing on the porch steps. Miss Holland, the headmistress, held a long cane in her hand, and it reminded Doris of the one that the horrible Nurse Hannah had used that fateful day.

"Right turn," Miss Holland ordered in a very loud voice. The kindy kids followed the principal's orders by imitating the older boys and girls. Then another command followed: "Quick march, left, right, left, right," called Miss Holland, beating the rhythm on the wall with her cane until the last student entered the school.

Mrs Brenchley led her new pupils to their desks which were large oaken ones that seated four students. Doris was placed in the row with Delores, Lena and Cliffie Ryder. Their classroom was large and combined two classes, standard one and standard two. Miss Holland taught from standard three upwards to standard seven. Doris was glad to hear the bell ringing to announce playtime. As the pupils filed out onto the playground, two of the working girls emerged from the dining room carrying trays of bread and jam for the school children. There were no drinks, the boys and girls had to make do with a drink of water from the tap in the change room, which was previously the hospital when the settlement was first established.

As the morning progressed Doris began to feel uncomfortable and restless. She needed to go to the toilet urgently but was too timid to ask her teacher if she could be excused. Instead she wet herself and started to cry. Delores called out loudly so that the whole class could hear, "Mrs Brenchley, Doris peed herself."

"Stella," Mrs Brenchley called to a girl who had been brought down with her sister Minette from Mulga Downs Station in the Pilbara, "take Doris up to the kindergarten and ask one of the girls to change her." When they returned Doris was still feeling embarrassed over the accident and vowed that she would ask to go to the toilet, even though it was almost two hundred yards behind the school. And she could always go behind the school or even under it. But she never wet in her bloomers again.

During play time one of the older girls joined in the games. Her name was Edna Roberts; she was a Wongi girl who came from Norseman, south of Kalgoorlie, and she asked the four little girls if they would like to go down to see the flooded river. Doris and Lena went cold all over and actually shivered as the memory came flashing back — it was exactly a year ago that they were tempted to do the same thing and they would never forget the consequences of their adventurous curiosity when Nurse Hannah caned them savagely. But before they could reply, the school bell rang and they all ran and formed a line in front of the school facing the porch where their teachers stood.

At lunchtime Edna Roberts was waiting for them outside, and insisted on escorting them to the dining room where they were given lunch of watery mutton stew, bread and butter and a mug of warm, sweet, milky tea. Edna waited outside on the verandah for all of the little ones to finish their lunch and when they formed a small group around her she asked, "who's coming down to the river?"

"Me," chorused Delores, Lillian Anderson and Marie Hannah from the Murchison region. Doris and Lena remained silent and refused to be coaxed into joining them on their sightseeing venture.

"You two coming or what?" asked Edna. In reply they shook their heads. "Well, at least come for a walk," she suggested.

This time Doris and Lena agreed to go for a walk with them. But when they reached the banks of the river, they realised that Edna Roberts had other ideas for them. Doris and Lena were expected to take risks like the rest of the group; they were not going to be treated as observers. Instead they were to become participants in this small venture. The two nervous girls stood on the muddy bank thinking that close-up the gushing torrent was even more fascinating. But it was also frightening. The sound of the swirling current as it collided with the trunks of the trees filled the air and blocked out any other sounds along the river banks. This increased their fascination of the threatening yet enchanting view spread out before them.

"Hey you two, you gunna stand there all day, or are you crossing the river like us," shouted Edna who was standing in the middle of the flowing river. Doris shivered as she said timidly, "I don't want to go into the water, I might fall over and get drowned." Lena agreed with Doris, and stepped back from the edge.

"Look at Delores, Lily and Marie," said Edna pointing to the girls who followed her into the rushing water. "They're not frightened like you two. See."

They had removed their bloomers and placed them on

their heads. The skirts of their woollen frocks were rolled up under their arms.

"You gunna come across here, or you want to stay by yourselves over there," challenged Edna.

"I'm coming," responded Lena as she stepped into the river. Doris realised that she had no choice but to follow. The panoramic view from the cliffs above didn't look as frightening as the sight from this angle. Up there it was fascinating. As Doris stood waiting, watching the others with their bloomers on top of their heads, their bare bottoms exposed and their frocks under their arms, scenes of them slipping and disappearing under the murky waters flashed before her.

"Come on, you're not going to drown," promised Edna.

The other three had nearly crossed to the other side. This gave Doris and Lena the courage they needed.

"It's cold," whispered Doris. There was no reply. It was not bad at first, but the further she went the deeper it got. When she reached the middle of the crossing, the river bed sloped slightly and the water level reached under her armpits and wet the hem of her frock.

All the girls were glad to reach the banks on the other side. Perhaps this was a rite of passage; if it was they had passed with flying colours, despite almost slipping in the ice-cold water. Fifteen minutes later all were dressed, and returned to the compound in time for school. But Doris was too uncomfortable to settle down to lessons because the hem of her pretty woollen frock was still wet. Mrs Brenchley noticed that she was fidgety. She walked over quietly and stood behind Doris, and said in her usual loud voice, "Have you wet yourself again?"

"No teacher," Doris softly replied.

"Well, what's wrong with you?" the teacher asked. "Why are you fidgeting? Stand up and speak up," she ordered. Doris stood up and tears welled up in her eyes as her teacher felt the hem of her frock.

"What happened to you?" shouted Mrs Brenchley. By this time the whole school, or at least these two classes, had stopped work to watch. Doris felt humiliated and shamed. Most of them felt sorry for her and the rest just watched. The tears spilled over her cheeks as her teacher asked, quietly this time, "What happened, and how did you get wet?"

"Crossing the river with Edna," she replied softly.

"Edna Roberts?" she asked.

"Yes, teacher," said Doris, rubbing her eyes with her small fists.

"Don't you ever leave the compound with anyone until school is finished. You hear that?"

"Yes, teacher," replied Doris. School was almost over so Doris remained in class. It wasn't necessary to send her up to the kindergarten to change. The childcare nurses would do that when she got home from school.

Doris refused to accompany Edna anywhere again. Instead she remained near her relations who were brought down to the settlement earlier. There were aunts like Nancy Matthews (Corry) from Walgun Station and the Doris sisters, and male relations who also became her protectors and to whom she became really attached.

True to her word Doris never left the compound until the end of the school year in December. But that half year at the big school was always remembered as the beginning of her formal education, a very special time.

* * *

The following year began with all the excitement and confusion that teachers all over the state and indeed the Commonwealth learned to cope with. The settlement school, as an Aboriginal community school, was more orderly and controlled because everyone knew each other, even the children who lived with their parents at the "camps", which were situated about five hundred yards west of the compound. The married couples returned to the settlement to allow the children to be educated, and the mothers to have their confinements and the delivery of their babies at the settlement hospital. Aboriginal children were not permitted to enrol at or attend any state or government schools, nor were their mothers admitted into district or maternity hospitals.

Doris was a clever child and displayed natural ability in reading and writing. She found mathematics very interesting but was hopeless at sketching and drawing. She was teased mercilessly because she could not pronounce her "r's". Quite often the pupils had to recite a verse of a poem. Doris loved poetry especially "From the Railway Carriage" by Robert Louis Stevenson, which began with:

Faster than fairies, faster than witches
Bridges and hedges, houses and ditches.

When Doris recited the poem all the "r's" were replaced by "w's". There was lots of snickering in the class room and mimicking in the playground. This caused so much embarrassment and, without her two kindergarten friends Andrew and Tony who had moved on to friendships with the older boys, Doris had to cope alone. So to overcome that speech problem she practised while she wandered around the compound by herself. Last year's kindergarten kids were now the new compound kids. That year her young aunt Nancy had left school and was learning to be a dressmaker, so Doris spent all day at the settlement sewing room.

Run rabbit, run rabbit, run, run, run.
Here comes the men with a gun, gun, gun.

She practised until she perfected the pronunciation. As an introverted timid child she hated having attention focused on her so for the rest of the term she concentrated on learning all that was offered in the school's curriculum.

That year and the following years proved to be rich and complete, so full of educational opportunities in Doris's journey of learning — despite the lack of other fundamental human rights that the wider Australian society enjoyed. The Aboriginal children's education standard was on the same par as any other primary state school in Western Australia. They were fortunate to have dedicated teachers like Mrs Brenchley and, as principal, Miss Holland's replacement, Mr Kau. These teachers never once told their students how privileged they were to be getting an education, they regarded it as a normal right enjoyed by all Australian children.

Besides acquiring literacy and numeracy skills Doris kept an eye on her daily timetable. She made sure she didn't miss those special lessons when she entered the world of fantasy through reading — she loved those stories of adventure, treachery and intrigue. She didn't mind if all the heroes were white and English like the Scarlet Pimpernel, Robin Hood and many, many more like them. These reading sessions sowed the seeds and nurtured her love for English literature and the English language.

The school was the focal point of the settlement. The adults were invited to all the activities and to come in any time to view the work done by the children. The annual school concert was attended by the whole community and usually occurred on the evening of the last day of the school year. Other than the concert, there were other normal events such as weddings, births and funerals and, of course, the seasonal changes that brought new games and recreational activities. These were influenced by the seasonal changes and the customs of the traditional owners, the Nyoongah people. After the first rains groups of children and an adult or two could be seen gathering mushrooms in the green fields and paddocks. They didn't have buckets so bark trays were used and when these bark trays were filled they were taken back to the cook who prepared all the luscious mushrooms in a frying pan with lots of dripping. This was accompanied by bread and warm sweet milky tea. But when the cold blustery winds blew over the settlement, the community stayed indoors — except the school children and the young people, recently graduated, who worked at tasks around the compound.

Winter coats or any sort of protective clothing were unavailable. Doris knew where all the small fire buckets were located. Her favourite fireplace was outside the woodshed near the bakery. One of her kinship aunts was the baker's girlfriend. After school Doris would make a beeline for the warm fire and a piece of damper, hot and fresh, spread with dripping. About mid morning the wind would ease and they would seek the warmth of the sun. But it was the old people and babies who were the most affected by the cold weather. Large numbers of babies died from chest infections and childhood diseases due to the fact that there were no antibiotics, immunisations or any suitable medications available.

The long walks to the cemetery became a regular event. With a child's funeral, the mourners would stand around the grave site to bid their last farewell and a special song would be sung as the coffin was lowered.

> There's a friend for little children,
> Above the bright blue skies,
> A friend who never changes
> A friend who never dies.
> Unlike a friend by nature
> Who changes with changing years,
> A friend who's always worthy
> Of the precious name He bears.

The next verse told about "A home for little children/ Above the bright blue skies ..." All the boys and girls who attended the funerals were comforted by the words of that special hymn and always left the cemetery with hope that when they died they would all go to that wonderful place in the skies.

Everyone hated the cold season when the rain ceased and the winds blew so cold that they seemed to come straight from the Antarctic Circle. Sometimes the howling winds that raged and circled under the eaves and gutterings were terrifying. The settlement community became less active and moved about like semi-frozen human beings.

Then, one morning, the incarcerated people would awaken to discover that the grey, depressing cover of gloom had been drawn back and flung beyond the clouds where it would remain until next winter. There would be blue skies and, as far as the eye could see, carpets of beautiful flowers covering the ground. There would be wild shrubs and bushes flaunting their beauty everywhere. It was with this reawakening of nature in all its exquisiteness that lessons in bush craft and survival skills began in earnest.

"You see this creeper," their Aboriginal tutors taught them, "you can dig bush potatoes." Or "pick these blossoms and shake them in your hands and suck up the sweet substance." Nancy and the other older girls demonstrated to the younger ones how to find bush foods by showing them and inviting them to taste, recognise and memorise. The lessons continued through spring and into summer. The boys and girls had a wonderful time searching for bush tucker and sampling different foods available from the bush supermarket. The boys learned how to use a ging or a shanghai and knew where every nest was located.

For Doris summer was exciting. She and the other children in her age group learned to swim and spent their days swimming in the pool. Being a compound kid was much better than being a kindy kid, there was freedom to wander around and to meet many other people.

Before they knew it Doris and her friends were answering the call of the school bell again. Mr Kau and Mrs Brenchley were anxious to begin teaching their old and their new pupils.

Sometimes there would be days when nothing other than

the usual, mundane things would happen. Then there were other times like when an aeroplane landed, or rather crashed, on One Mile Hill. It happened during the night and created so much interest that every man, woman and child had to see it, including Doris. So after school every student went to see the crashed plane. Doris touched the cold, twisted metal and shivered. She couldn't understand. The next day two of the big boys Henry Ford and Eric Conway, who were in short pants at the time, decided to paint the Royal Australian Air Force insignia, a circle in red, white and royal blue, on their knees. They were punished by the head-mistress for using crayons in that manner, by a caning on both hands several times. They didn't cry, but big tears filled Doris's eyes and spilled down her cheeks. Everyone at the settlement knew that they were related. Eric came from Mulga Downs Station near Marble Bar in the Pilbara, and Henry was a son of her cousin from Wiluna in the Upper Murchison. They were two of her "minders". After school the two lads were teased and taunted by the older girls. They all grouped together and sang a song that was popular during the Charleston era —

Roll 'em boys, roll 'em
Roll 'em boys and show your pretty knees.

Henry and Eric, with their hands over their ears, ran for cover. It was some time before the teasing stopped.

It wasn't long after the plane crash, during morning playtime, that a strange sound was heard. It seemed to be coming from up the road near the hospital.

"What's that?" asked the younger children.

All eyes were focused on the gravel road that led into the

settlement. They didn't have to wait long before they saw the cause of the noise.

"Look," said Michael Robinson, "it's army trucks."

"Army trucks?" said one of the senior boys, "what are they coming here for?"

None of these children had ever known or experienced the effects of war. However, all the school children knew what soldiers were; as in schools all over Australia, special days were commemorated and remembered. The whole school looked forward to the Anzac memorial service that was broadcast to schools including the Moore River Aboriginal Settlement School.

The school also held its own service when the local community was invited to participate. Every year the children sang:

> We will remember them today,
> Who from their homelands sailed away,
> So proudly and so willingly,
> They gave their lives for you and me
> Hear their quiet sleeping.

They would leave the service feeling sad and reflecting on the soldiers who had died fighting a war overseas to make Australia a safer place to live.

The pupils watched in awe as the military trucks came closer. The leading truck stopped near the first group of children and a soldier shouted in a very loud voice, "Where is Mr Leeming, the superintendent?"

"Over there," they replied, pointing to the office. The boys and girls watched with great interest and curiosity as the convoy of five trucks followed the leading vehicle and pulled up outside the small office. The "ding, dong" of the school bell brought the children back to reality. They found it hard to concentrate on their lessons during the rest of the afternoon so, as soon as school was over, everyone raced down to see where the visitors were. Some of the children followed the road around while others took a short cut between the staff quarters and the girls dormitories.

The army was setting up a camp on the edge of the pine plantation, in no time at all the tents were pitched in neat rows. As the settlement was ten miles up the Moore River from its mouth, the soldiers may have been guarding the coast and patrolling for any Japanese invaders.

Having the army at the settlement created lots of interest and fired up the boys' imaginations. All the children were inspired to invent new games when the soldiers dug a huge trench in the bottom of the kindergarten playground. Doris and her friends had hours of fun playing there, unaware of the real purpose of the trench.

The mothers continued to meet and sit near the fence under the pine trees, but now it was because there was a chance of meeting a "soldier boy". The settlement community became used to the sound of bugle calls echoing across the valley.

One day Doris was taken by an older relative to meet her "soldier boy", but more importantly for Doris, it was the opportunity to taste army food — biscuits, tinned meat, and chocolates. The rendezvous was arranged to take place in the afternoon, so young Doris was having her usual nap while her cousin and the boyfriend were making love.

There was a barbed-wire fence prison hastily erected at the

army camp by the soldiers. An Aboriginal man was incarcerated there and members of the settlement community were forbidden to go anywhere near the prison. No one knew what his offence was or whether he was charged and sentenced under military law or common law.

One day all the members of the settlement community were invited by the army to ride in the back of the trucks towards the coast. This was most enjoyable, the boys and girls remembered the incident for many days to come. It was a few days later when, quite unexpectedly, the settlement community awoke to discover that sometime during the night the Army had dismantled their camp and moved away and were never seen around there again. The barbed-wire prison and the deep trench in the playground were the only reminders that they were ever at the Moore River Native Settlement.

* * *

When the settlement was opened the first intake was brought down from the Pilbara. That was the region where part-Aboriginal children were being born to Mardu or Aboriginal women most frequently. The Department of Native Affairs monitored the movement of the mothers and their children and when they thought the time was right they removed the children under ministerial warrants and sent them down to the Moore River Native Settlement. Although Doris and her sister Anna were not brought down under those circumstances they were still regarded as family under the kinship system where boys and girls had obligations to care for and protect the younger ones.

Doris, the youngest of the group, was one of the Pilbara

children who was rather spoilt by the older relations. Not all of them were blood relations but that didn't matter. Because of the strong kinship system they became her substitute brothers and sisters, which meant that both groups were responsible for her well-being and safety. Doris had the choice of who she accompanied on walks and other kinds of outings. Spring seemed to be the season for life and romance. She often became their companion when her aunts or older cousins went courting down the river side. Doris played quietly on the banks of the river while the couples made love in a secluded place protected by thick shrubs. She was always instructed to "sing out" if anybody was approaching.

When Doris saw her "big" brothers Henry, Eric, Jim O'Connors and Arnold Franks standing together in a group talking, she knew that they were planning something. "I want to come for a walk with you, Henry," pleaded Doris. She knew that if she went with them, she wouldn't have to walk, because they would take turns carrying her.

"No, you can't come this time," said Henry. "Go and find your auntie Nancy."

"You stay here and we'll bring you something back."

"I want to come with you," she cried, stamping her feet. The four lads stood in a circle whispering amongst themselves.

"All right you can come, but you have to go to the store first and get some things for us," Henry said. Doris agreed and took the money. She ran as fast as she could to the store where she bought a packet of Kraft cheese, a bar of chocolate and a packet of milk arrowroot biscuits. But when she arrived at the pine tree where the four lads were supposed to be waiting, no one was there, they were gone. She called out to them, "Henry, Eric, Jimmo," but there was no reply. Doris wandered around the compound until she found someone with whom she could share the food. She had no idea that the four young men had plans of their own and they certainly didn't include minding a little girl. They had appointments with four pretty young women that they were very anxious to keep.

Soon spring faded onto summer and the new year heralded the new school year. The numbers remained the same, about fifty school children. There were not many changes except that some of the senior boys and girls were sent out to work. Henry joined his mother Molly and her husband, his step-father Norman Michaels, a Nyoongah man, on Shannaway Farm about eight miles east of the settlement, not far from the mouth of the Moore River.

Sister Kathleen Jones, an Anglican nun, replaced Sister Eileen who was transferred to the Forest River in the far north. Sister Kathleen was an Aboriginal woman from Wiluna but who grew up elsewhere. At the end of the second term, ten of the junior girls were chosen to go on a camping trip with Sister Kathleen on Shannaway Farm. The farm supplied the settlement community with vegetables, eggs, and rockmelons and watermelons.

They travelled on the back of the settlement truck and pitched their tents on the banks of the river. It was a wonderful experience. Molly and Norman Michaels and the working boys visited the camp every night. They told stories — but definitely not any ghost stories, they were warned.

The highlight of the camp was when they were invited by Mr Duncan to visit the farm and see all the baby ducklings and chickens. After their excursion to the farm the ten girls walked up to a large turnip patch to do some weeding. The sun was warm on their backs, they worked all day, pausing for a picnic lunch of boiled eggs, bread and butter and billy tea. This was prepared by Sister Kathleen's assistants, Edna Robinson and Joan Cameron, who also cooked the meals on an open fire.

On the way back to their camp they called in to the large farm house where the Michaels and the working boys lived. Sister Kathleen was Molly's cousin, so the two had a lot to talk about. After a delicious meal of beef stew and damper, they walked home to their camp escorted by the farm labourers. That night, after a warm sponge over, all went to bed and had a peaceful sleep. They wished they could stay there for a long, long time. Doris and her friends caught fish in the river and cooked them on the coals and generally enjoyed themselves. The wildflowers were in full bloom and the green fields spread out for miles.

Unfortunately their holidays were cut short when the farm manager Mr Duncan came down with a message that the settlement community needed the two older girls because all the working girls were in hospital suffering with "the dandelion fever" (influenza). The tents were dismantled and everything packed and ready when Mr Duncan came to pick them up in his white ute. There were no antibiotics or treatments available at the settlement hospital for influenza. Most of the adults recovered but some of the old people and young babies were not so fortunate.

It was at this time Doris noticed that there were changes happening around the settlement. Tony and Andrew's mother came and took them home to Geraldton where she had a husband and a home. Families from the camps were leaving, anyone over sixteen was hurriedly sent out to work, including her auntie Nancy; numbers were decreasing almost daily. The school children didn't worry too much about that, people were always coming and going.

One day after rollcall in the dormitory an announcement was made by Nurse Joyce Truman: "The settlement will be closing down and the boys and girls will be sent to Christian missions."

The Government had decided to abolish their protection policy and introduce a new policy — of assimilation. This meant that all Indigenous peoples of this country would be expected to achieve and maintain the same living standards as those in the wider Australian society. The Aboriginal children were to be absorbed into mainstream Australia and were to be treated equally as Australian citizens. To achieve this ultimate goal the children must be brought up by persons who already believe that "Jesus loved the little children, all the children of the world". It was decided that an ideal environment must be created so that this theory could be put into practice. The settlement life would end, making way for the establishment of Christian missions throughout the state.

The final day of the school year came and the school song was sung for the last time.

Now our school is over
And we are going home,

Goodbye, Goodbye —
We will be kind and true,
Goodbye, Goodbye,
We will be kind and true.

That evening the school concert and a Christmas party were held; these were not to be missed. Father Christmas came down the gravel road on a sleigh pulled by two mules. There were cheers from the children, who had never seen Santa Claus riding on a sleigh. The whole community was abuzz with excitement. When the concert was performed and delightfully received, Santa handed out Christmas presents, there were toys for all the boys and girls. Doris and all the other girls were given beautiful rag dolls with celluloid faces and different coloured hair made from yellow, black and brown wool. These dolls were made by Mrs Brenchley, Miss Chapman, the infants teacher, and Mrs Kau, the wife of the principal, who taught crafts and embroidery.

The Christmas atmosphere filled the school hall which doubled as a classroom during the school year. The teaching staff, the administration staff, parents and friends sat in their chairs and watched the children enjoy themselves. This was their special night. Amid the noise, the colourful balloons and streamers above, it was impossible to sit still for more than a few minutes. The children were weaving in and out on the crowded floor, stopping to compare presents. With their little tummies filled with lollies, lemonade, cakes and ice-cream, all the children were as happy as could be.

Then a loud voice called out amid the din, "Silence everyone," and there was instant silence throughout the hall.

"Now boys and girls, sit down and be very, very quiet,"

ordered Mr Kau the headmaster. When everyone was seated, all eyes were focused on Mr Kau who acted as the Master of Ceremonies. "Now Kim is going to sing a song called 'Meet Me in St Louis'." Kim was the son of one of the officials who was representing the Native Affairs Department in Perth. This song was followed by items performed by the settlement's carpenter and his family, the Scanlons, who sang songs like "Cruising Down the River on a Sunday Afternoon" and several other popular songs of the time. Doris could have listened all night as their voices filled the whole room. The Scanlons sang in perfect harmony and won many fans that night. That final concert performed by the staff and their children who were on holidays from boarding schools in Perth was a perfect ending to the most memorable Christmas-tree party in the history of the settlement.

"This is our last Christmas at Moore River," said one of the senior girls sadly.

"And it was our best one," answered her friend. It would be remembered for a long, long time. The girls have never had dolls in their entire lives; they loved them so much that they decided that they would never let them out of their sight. With cheers and wishes for "a merry Christmas" still ringing in her ears Doris was too excited to sleep, so she and her friends sat on the edge of their beds and reflected on the evening's events.

The next day the settlement community was told details of the Government's decision to close the institution and transfer the children to a Christian mission somewhere down south. The whole community had difficulty understanding and accepting that decision. What a contrast to the celebrations of joy and happiness of last night was the sense of despair and hopelessness today.

"The Government is taking our children away again," cried the unhappy mothers. What was hurting them was the knowledge that there was nothing they could do about it. Their feelings were not even considered.

The Department of Native Affairs had already set the wheels in motion for this change. The number of adults had been decreasing for some time. Now many were encouraged to marry their sweethearts and move to the husband's place of employment, with the promise that their children would be able to join them when they had made a "proper" home like that of the white person. The parents left with a strong determination to work hard to bring their living standards up to the Department's expectations so that they would be able to have their children live with them. Meanwhile the boys and girls would live at the mission and remain as wards of the state with the Commissioner of Native Affairs as their legal guardian.

For the next few weeks the seamstresses were extremely busy making frocks for the girls who, for the first time in their lives, were allowed to choose from the bolts of materials that filled the shelves of the sewing room. They were told to choose fabric for two frocks, one for best and one for second best. The girls already had school tunics with different coloured blouses for each age group. The tunics were made from a very strong striped cotton material, brown blouses for the senior girls, blue for the junior girls and pink for the lower primary girls. Doris's auntie Nancy made her frocks.

Doris went down every day to watch the development from the cutting table to the finished products.

* * *

One day while she was sitting by herself on the verandah sewing a marble bag from remnants of pretty material given to her by one of the seamstresses, a Nyoongah woman named Ruby called out to her, "Doris, come here."

Doris stood up and glanced at the door of the sewing room, then ran over to the young woman.

"You want to come for a walk with me?" asked Ruby.

"Yeah, I want to come with you," she replied as soon as she noticed that the woman had a parcel of food in her hand.

"Wait here," she told Doris, "while I tell Nancy that we're going dinner out." Ruby went into the sewing room and told Nancy where they were going.

"Alright," replied Nancy, "I'll see you this afternoon." She was actually relieved that her niece was going somewhere. Nancy was one of Doris's substitute mothers and since they were told of the transfer Doris had become rather clingy. Doris and Ruby set off past the dairy and disappeared amongst a dense thicket of tangled creepers that grew along the banks of the river. Ruby and her young companion crossed the river then followed the fence line on the other side.

"You want a piggy back?" asked Ruby.

"No, I'm not tired yet," Doris answered softly. She had learned never to ask adults about their business or the reasons for their actions, she just walked quietly behind them until they reached their destination. Small as she was, she loved bush walks.

Suddenly, as they approached a clump of mallee trees they heard a sound very familiar to Doris, it was the neighing of a horse. She froze.

"It's all right. Don't be frightened," said Ruby in her quiet comforting manner. "You know Gycie?" pointing to the man mounted on a small horse. To Doris it looked more like a pony.

Gycie dismounted and kissed Ruby who was his girlfriend, then removed the saddle and rug from his horse and placed them on the ground. After lunch he replaced the saddle and blanket then picked Doris up and plonked her on the animal's neck. The lovers climbed up behind her. Doris loved the sensation of riding on the animal's bare back.

Ruby's boyfriend Gycie was declared an outlaw by the settlement officials and was banned from the place. But that didn't stop him and Ruby from having regular rendezvous at designated spots around the settlement boundaries. The food and the warm sun made Doris sleepy. The pair of lovers decided to rest in a clearing in the banksia thicket where they left Doris sleeping on the saddle on the ground near the horse while they went off in the bushes nearby to make love. Doris had no idea why Gycie was called an outlaw, important issues were discussed by adults only. She awakened just before the lovers came back. Before returning to the compound Ruby swore Doris to secrecy.

* * *

During the weekend Doris realised that she forgot to tell her relations in the "native" camp about the big move. There were two such camps in different locations. There was a Wongi camp for the people who came from the Eastern

Goldfields region, and the other one that was frequented by Doris was located on the opposite side where the old army camp had been. The school children were still forbidden to make any contact with the "natives" but Doris and her older relations found a way to visit them without getting caught breaking the rules. Doris spent at least one day a week with these Mardu people who came down from the Pilbara region for medical treatment at the Royal Perth Hospital, then transferred to the settlement to convalesce. When discharged they were returned to their homelands. It was from these people that she learned who her parents were and where to find them.

"When you grow up you look for your Mummy," her old jumu told her. The day before the girls departed Doris visited the camp to say goodbye to the people there. There was a strange woman amongst them. Her name was Gracie Toby and she came from Nullagine.

"Your Mummy and Daddy still there at Baffa Danns Station," she told Doris who paid little attention and wasn't too interested at the time. But she nodded politely and said nothing but changed the subject to talk about her new dresses, underwear and real swimming bathers. That visit was the last contact with Mardu people that she would have for many years.

The next day Doris and twenty-two girls were seated on the back of the truck talking quietly amongst themselves, wondering where they were going to end up. Those who remained, the working girls, stood around reassuring the others, "We'll come down to see you."

"Alright," they chorused, "don't forget now." The waving

and the shouts of "goodbye" continued until the settlement was out of sight. Then there was a hush as each girl became a solitary person saying her silent farewells to her special places through the countryside where she had learned bush lore and cultural lessons. As they travelled along the gravel road with the thick dust rising all around them, each girl pointed out where special events and incidents had taken place.

The women and girls of the settlement community looked forward to the winter and spring, the seasons when bush foods were gathered and taken back and shared amongst the incarcerated people. Doris was always fascinated with the wildflowers that grew around the settlement, an important part of the heathlands of Western Australia renowned for some of this country's most beautiful and unusual wildflowers. She loved to touch and pick the beautiful kangaroo paws, the myrtles, the smoke bush and the banksia. In the spring time when the bush was ladened with blossoms and their fragrance filled the air, the women took great pleasure in teaching the girls the Nyoongah names of the flowers and shrubs, and how to search for and identify edible plants. Those days were the most enjoyable and Doris got so much pleasure she wished the season would never end. But end it did. It was time to move on. The gathering of traditional foods would remain a wonderful memory.

Doris glanced around at her travelling companions and recalled how, after Christmas, they had carried around with them all the time those beautiful dolls with the celluloid faces. The dolls were taken everywhere, down to the river and into the dormitories — in fact, where the girls went the

dolls went also. One day they wondered where the dolls'
pretty faces had disappeared to — they were covered in dirt.
There was only one thing to do and that was to wash them.
But, alas, when they washed their dolls' faces the features
disappeared completely, so all the dolls were left on the
creepers to dry, and were left behind.

Familiar places passed, with little interest, Doris was far
more intrigued with the changing scenery, especially with
the large bracken fern growing profusely along the railway
tracks beside the road.

It was late afternoon when they reached the destination
planned for them by the Department of Native Affairs. It
came as a surprise, the girls were led to believe that they were
being sent to a Christian mission. Instead, they arrived and
unloaded their belongings from the truck at the Campbell
Barracks, an army camp in Swanbourne, a suburb of Perth,
right near the coast. Most of the girls had never seen the
ocean before so this was a delightful experience which
evoked in Doris a deep respect and affection for the sea. She
loved everything about it. Unbeknown to the girls from
Moore River, the girls from Carrolup Settlement were due to
meet up with them soon. The idea was that these girls from
the two settlements should get to know each other better
before they all arrived at their new home, the Roelands
Mission.

Those weeks in Perth were filled with all kinds of pleasant
activities. Doris and her friends went sightseeing, visiting the
South Perth zoo and having picnics on the banks on the Swan
River, but what she liked most was going to a cinema where
she saw the film *Eureka Stockade*. She didn't understand it

then but nonetheless she still enjoyed the action. Films and
the ocean were the positive images of Perth that remained
with her always.

Then one day a huge bus drove into Campbell Barracks
followed by a car driven by an official from the Department.
And surprise, surprise! Doris's auntie Nancy and two working
girls got out. Nancy had come to say goodbye to her niece
and the rest of the girls from Moore River. She looked
beautiful in her new clothes and sandals. And there were
tearful goodbyes to those twenty-nine Roman Catholic girls
who departed on a big bus driven by a priest to their final
destination, the Wandering Mission near Narrogin south-
east of Perth. The remaining seventeen were Anglicans, who
travelled down south with the Carrolup girls to wait at Carrolup Settlement until the Roelands Mission sent for them.
Carrolup Settlement was similar in structure to Moore River
so it didn't take long for Doris and her group to settle in.
Besides, there was a couple there who used to live at Moore
River who elected themselves as her substitute parents. They
were Minnie and Alf Merrit who had both worked with
Doris's mother Molly in the kitchen before she absconded
in 1941. The hot, dry summer days at Carrolup were eventless
after the holidays spent in Perth. There were not too many
places to see or things to do — except swimming in the small
river hole.

While the girls were idly sitting in the shade of the red
gums or under the weeping willow trees sharing stories and
food, the Moore River boys were swimming down at the
beach and sightseeing in Perth. As soon as the boys returned
to Carrolup with the truck, the girls and their belongings

were loaded on to the back and they began the last leg of their journey south to Roelands. The boys would follow Doris's group later, with the Catholic boys going to Wandering Mission and the Anglican boys to Roelands.

So at midday on 11 January 1950 Doris and thirty-one other girls who were transferred from Moore River and Carrolup Native Settlements arrived at the Roelands Native Mission. Missions were vitally necessary to provide spiritual and moral guidance to native children — particularly to part-Aboriginal children, according to Mr F.I. Bray, who succeeded A.O. Neville as Commissioner of Native Affairs and guardian to all Aboriginal children in 1940. A.O. Neville was the government official in 1931, then known as Protector of Aborigines, who had pursued Molly across the state. The title may have changed but the control over Aboriginal people's lives had not.

CHAPTER 9

Faith, Hope and Charity

"And now abideth faith hope and charity, these three, but the greatest of these is charity."

1 Corinthians 13:13.

F ROM THE BACK OF THE TRUCK the unvarying countryside of the south-west was becoming monotonous, featuring dry paddocks where sheep and cattle grazed in whatever shade was available. The summer scenery changed only when the paddocks were separated by uncleared bushland, a refreshing break in the passing views of settled landscapes. Then at last the truck slowed down and the driver made a sharp left turn onto the dirt road that would lead Doris and her travelling companions to their final destination, the Roelands Native Mission.

They reached the mission boundary soon enough, their access blocked by a gate. While the driver's offsider climbed down to open it, Doris was able to read the large noticeboard that told new arrivals they were entering the Mission Farm and underneath was a text from the New Testament, the one

where Jesus told the parents who bought their infants to be
blest by Him: "Suffer the little children to come unto me and
forbid them not, for such is the kingdom of God." Luke
18:16.

What a contrast from the landscape that they had travelled
through, to come to this place where there were fields of
green potato plants and an avenue of wild walnut trees. They
drove across a small bridge, up a very steep hill where they
reached a cross roads. Turning left, the truck driver stopped
in front of a building, which Doris discovered later was the
Roelands' kitchen and dining room.

It was midday and the sun was beating down on their
unprotected heads. Doris and her companions remained
seated, watching as a man walked towards them down the
gravel road.

"I'm Ken Cross, the superintendent of the mission," he
told the driver as he shook his hand. Then he took the driver
aside and said in a low voice, "What do you mean thirty-two
girls?" shaking his head in disbelief.

"Yes, there are thirty-two," the driver answered firmly.

"We were expecting twenty-two, we certainly don't have
room for another ten."

"I can't take them back," said the driver.

"No, and I don't want to send them back," responded the
superintendent. He realised that he was in a dilemma that
needed fixing immediately. "Tell the girls to get off and wait
in the shade near that building," he told the driver as he
pointed to a mud brick hut.

So while Mr Cross left to call an urgent meeting of all the
missionaries, the Carrolup truck was emptied of its cargo of

young girls and the cardboard boxes which held their clothes. Then the truck was reversed back onto Mission Road and soon disappeared around the corner in a cloud of dust. Doris and the rest of the group did as they were instructed, and sat and waited patiently for someone to come for them.

Time seemed to drag on forever and the group of new-comers started to become restless. Doris and her friends from Moore River decided to explore their nearby surroundings.

"What are those bushes growing in the creek?" asked Marie.

"That's blackberry bushes," replied Inez.

"Are they good to eat?" asked Doris.

"Yes, they're really good to eat."

The curious girls all climbed through the fence and picked a few ripe blackberries and took them back to the shade to eat them. They weren't too bad. Not as sweet as mulberries, but they were edible. The group had finished the berries and there was still no sign of any staff member. The girls from Carrolup had run out of patience and all of them decided to run away back to where they came from. Doris and the rest of the group remained in the shade, resting and watched the girls proceed down the bank, through the fence and up the steep hillside to the other side. Then there came a sound of heavy boots on the gravel road, followed by the loud voices of men.

"Hey you girls, come back here!"

"Come on, hurry up," one of them ordered. The would-be runaways were herded back by the working boys who were home on holidays. They told the girls to sit down and be patient. "It won't be long now."

As the large red gums cast their long shadows over the dining room the girls were instructed to follow Miss Vincent, a Wongi missionary, to the junior girls' wash house and bathroom where they were ordered one by one to sit on a chair to have their lovely long locks trimmed. Their hair was cut very short, an inch above the ears. When the girls saw the results some swore loudly and abused the untrained barber, others — like Doris — were silent, their heart filled with an anger that they wished they could express, but couldn't, suffering in silence while others cried. Then they were bathed in disinfectant and their heads deloused with kerosene, the smell of which filled the small bathroom, almost choking them. "Cleanliness is next to Godliness" was the first important lesson that Doris and the thirty-one other Aboriginal girls learned that day. When the cleansing and delousing process was completed the girls were formed into two groups according to age and size, then shown to their new homes.

All of the girls were immediately categorised into two explicit groups, the "old" girls and the "new" girls. Animosity and competitiveness were encouraged by the missionaries, perhaps unknowingly, but nevertheless it created a very tense atmosphere in what should have been an example of a Christian institution as a home of peace and contentment.

* * *

Roelands Native Mission was formerly known as Seven Hills Chandler Boys Home, and was owned and established by Albany Bell, a philanthropist and businessman. It was based on an idea conceived by T.C. Chandler and therefore was

known as the Chandler Boys Scheme. It was one of the
private organisations attempting to help the unemployed
youth. The Great Depression caused most of the Australian
population to change their way of life and adapt an alternative one. It was the mid 1930s and there was high unemploy-
ment throughout the nation and a large number were the
youth of Western Australia, teenagers who were living in
poverty with no hope for a better future. Many were school
leavers who had missed out on apprenticeships and other
training and educational programs.

The Chandler Boys Scheme was seen as a ray of hope for
at least some of these teenagers during the early years of the
Depression. It attracted a great deal of attention from the
public whose generous donations helped fund it as a farm
school where boys could learn and develop agricultural
skills, such as market gardening. The scheme closed in 1937
after only four years of operation.

The property then reverted to Mr Bell. The idea of a "farm
settlement" for the Indigenous people of the south-west of
Western Australia was given some consideration by this chari-
table man. He saw the opportunity to do something about
the plight of the Aboriginal people in the area, "when so
much criticism is in the air with regard to the treatment of
the natives," Albany Bell told a reporter of the *West Australian*
newspaper in 1937. He said that the business and general
communities who made generous contributions to the Chandler Boys Home would be gratified to know that the money
would help to "discharge some of our obligations towards
the native race," and this experiment would be watched with
interest.

Mr Bell contacted A.O. Neville, the Commissioner of Native Affairs, and presented him with a very special request for orphans between the ages of six and eight years of age for the Roelands Native Mission. He wanted a list of those attending the kindergarten and the school at Moore River Native Settlement. He received a reply from the Commissioner informing him that: "I have been through the lists and there are very few children of the type required."

The only suitable children available, according to Mrs Brenchley the school teacher, were children of Aboriginal mothers and white fathers. Mr Bell decided to take those children who were nominated by the Commissioner and, in 1937, the first intake of Aboriginal children was transferred from Moore River Settlement to the Roelands Native Mission farm. They were to be cared for by Christian missionaries because: "They have the native's spiritual, moral and material welfare at heart and we believe that they can guide the natives to independence," wrote Royal Commissioner M.D. Moseley in a report of 24 January 1935.

* * *

Now, thirteen years after the first intake, on 11 January 1950, Doris and the thirty-one other girls were transferred from the Carrolup Native Settlement, making this the third group of children to be admitted to the Roelands Mission.

While most of the girls were lamenting the loss of their beautiful locks, Doris was far more interested in where they were going to live than what she looked like. She followed the others, most of whom had both hands covering the wide bare strip above their ears and all smelling strongly of kerosene. The odour followed them like an invisible cloud and they breathed the fumes through their nostrils as they walked across the playing field.

Doris felt as though the surrounding hills were suffocating her, as there were no distant fields or wide open spaces. The Roelands Native Mission farm was nestled amongst seven hills in a fertile valley. Doris paused for a second to get a better view of her new home. She saw that it was totally different from the two government settlements she had previously been in. This place was small and the buildings were built in a circle, and there was a road in the centre of the mission with large playing fields on either side. There were shady trees on the hillsides, but the parched earth in that late summer month gave the place the feeling of a quiet, sleepy village.

"Come on Doris, don't stand there," called out Marie. "Hurry up."

"Alright, I'm coming," answered Doris, as she rejoined the group. The girls were led to a large cottage where they were greeted by an elderly couple, Mr and Mrs Syd Williams.

"Come this way," said Mrs Williams as she led the way onto a large verandah. "You can choose any bed, and put your belongings underneath it for now," she told the group. "We'll sort out everything tomorrow."

The sound of a cow bell rang out across the field. "That's the kitchen bell, go and wash your face and hands and follow the other girls down to the dining hall," Mrs Williams told them. The group bunched up together and walked down for tea.

To twelve-year-old Doris the segregation of boys and girls was most upsetting, but to siblings it was devastating. Entering the dining hall the boys and girls formed two lines and marched in singing:

Steadily forward march to Jesus we will bring
Sinners of every kind the Lord will take them in …
The rich, the poor as well, it doesn't matter who
So bring them in with all their sins …

The settlement girls thought that was directed at them, and felt very uncomfortable — like they were the little heathens who needed evangelising. Doris for one felt out of place in this spotlessly clean dining room with its snow white curtains and wooden floors that shone like glass. The curtains had words on the frills, words like "Peace", "Joy", "Truth", "Faith", "Hope", and "Love". She had never seen anything like this before. Doris and her friends took their places opposite the local girls, four on either side of the table. The food was different to what they had been used to, it was wholesome and fresh. The meal served that evening was bread and butter, fresh fruit and a piece of cheese.

From that day onwards Doris and the other girls from the settlements had to learn self control and discipline, in this place there would be no more eating between meals and definitely no damper and tea to be shared. It would be strictly bread and butter and tea with breakfast, and milk or tea with supper. Doris and her friends were referred to as the "new" girls which created division and animosity between them and the other girls. The two groups became highly competitive, each wanting to prove that they were the best in any aspect of life on the mission. Those so-called Christian girls never came to Doris and her friends to introduce themselves, their reception was very cold indeed. They never stopped to think that it was very difficult or even traumatic for those separated from parents and other members of their families left behind at Moore River or Carrolup. The missionaries were unaware that they had instigated and encouraged the rivalry between the two groups, not only by labelling them, but by giving the new girls special treatment.

Doris discovered later that not all the girls were unfeeling, but it was mainly the original group of mission girls who made comments like: "Everything was good until the new girls came here." Doris couldn't understand why someone would resent other Aboriginal girls sharing a home with them. Perhaps these "old" girls felt threatened now that they had to share their substitute parents, and their small-minded community was disrupted. These "old" girls hardly ever or maybe never had any contact with Aboriginal people and they had become isolated and alienated from their own people. Many were theoretically government-manufactured orphans and now that their mission foster parents had opened their arms wide to embrace Doris and her friends, they didn't like that one bit.

The latest additions to the mission family could still be identified as the girls not wearing white aprons. The rivalry continued for at least a couple of months until the differences became obscure and were forgotten. Soon all the girls wore white aprons. The white aprons had pockets, which became useful for not only keeping hankies in, but for carrying anything like unwanted vegetables from their plates that could be thrown in the rubbish bin later. The uniform white aprons gave the girls a new identity, but they still had a long way to go before they could become totally accepted by the other girls.

The task of assimilating them into the mission began the first week when Mr Cross welcomed them during morning devotion, which was held after breakfast every day.

"Now what I would like all the 'new' girls to do," he paused and looked around the dining room then continued, "I mean the intermediate and senior girls ... I want them to learn and memorise Psalm 1, verses 1 to 6," he said slowly, holding up his black leather Bible. "And when you know it by heart, I want you to stand up and recite it in front of everyone at morning devotion." He gazed around the dining hall expecting to see a glimpse of a reaction; receiving none he announced that they would receive a reward for their efforts, a copy of the New Testament. He showed them a sample. It was a slim volume in black leather with bold gold letters.

Later, when all of the girls had successfully recited the passage and received their prizes, Mr Cross presented them with another challenge, and that was to read and memorise a longer portion of scripture. This time it took a bit longer. It was the section 1 Corinthians 13: 1–13 where Paul in his letter to the Corinthian Christians said that faith, hope and charity were important factors in their lives, that charity means to have patience, be humble and serve others without expecting any rewards. Charity means pure love, a love that exceeds and rises above almost everything. Doris enjoyed reading the Bible and learning this chapter most; it was poetic and rhythmic. So she tried very hard to overcome her nervousness so that she wouldn't make any mistakes or miss verses when it was her turn to recite.

After that, different verses and Bible stories were told, but the messages and subject matter were always the same, making Doris and her friends fully aware that they were "ungodly" and "unrighteous". They were bombarded with negative references because of their spiritual status, or rather their non-Christian one. This attitude fed their low self-esteem, so while they were in this vulnerable position, the conditioning and the Christian indoctrination began in earnest. Within a couple of years most of Doris's friends were converted to Christianity, except Doris and a couple of others who were still resisting the zeal and endeavour of the missionaries.

The method of alternating negative and positive teachings from the Bible only confused them. In spite of how well-planned and skillfully executed the lessons were, it wasn't until the Easter convention the following year that Doris accepted the Lord as her Saviour. Pastor Reginald Wright showed her in simplistic terms that Jesus loved her and that he never set himself up on a pedestal, but was a humble man who was a sinner saved by grace.

From day one she had been taught that the mission was based on faith, hope and charity, but the big question was how does one so young as Doris define these emotions and feelings. Although she was unable to express them in words she could understand them by believing in the Christian faith, its virtues and principles, and most of all by the power of prayer.

Prayers and praying were an important part of mission life.

Hope, on the other hand, was carried in her heart every day, it replaced the word "wish". Doris learned that in the mission you did not wish for things to happen, but you hoped and prayed that they would.

That Easter there was rejoicing and celebrations, but most importantly there was praise and thanksgiving to the Lord that the missionaries through their faith had had their prayers answered. The joy had spread throughout the mission like an epidemic, it was at this time that all the girls became united through Christ and their belief in Christianity.

* * *

A new dormitory was built for the girls and the responsibility for this new building was given to a retired hospital matron Matron Mildred Murray, a spinster with whom Doris was to have many clashes. Matron had taken over the responsibility of the dormitory from Mr and Mrs Syd Williams.

At that time Roelands Native Mission Farm had the largest grapefruit orchard in the state. Doris had never seen a grapefruit until one day, while she was working at the home of one of the missionaries, she noticed a big round yellow fruit.

"What is that?" she asked.

"That's a grapefruit. Haven't you seen one before?" her workmate responded with a rather disbelieving expression on her face.

"No," replied Doris as she returned to her chores. That must be the most delicious fruit in the whole wide world, she thought. She loved eating sweet, juicy grapes and so couldn't wait to taste her first grapefruit. Doris was given a grapefruit one morning and what a disappointment that was! It wasn't sweet and juicy, rather it was sour and juicy — although, once she got used to it, she rather enjoyed it.

During grapefruit season the mission relied heavily on the boys and girls to pick, wash and pack the fruit ready to be transported to the local markets in the city and for marketing overseas to Singapore. This was the most enterprising activity on the Roelands Farm. At that time of the year all capable mission teenagers were required during grapefruit season. All the farm jobs and domestic work were done by the boys and girls with a senior to supervise. This meant they worked six hours a day, six days a week. Sunday was set aside for worship and meditation.

It was a life of firm discipline and hard labour, a regimented lifestyle, which was so different to the kind Doris was used to at Moore River Settlement. At first it was difficult for Doris to cope with the restriction and the segregation. All movement was controlled, walks in the bush or anywhere off the mission had to be approved by the staff and, most importantly, in the company of an adult. All correspondence was monitored and censored.

Segregation was a policy introduced by the missionaries to prevent any promiscuous or inappropriate behaviour between the young men and women. It meant that Doris and the other settlement girls could not fulfill their cultural obligations to their brothers. One girl dared to greet her older brother with a hug in full view of a certain missionary. For this she was sent out to work as a domestic help as soon as there was a position available. She was just fourteen.

As soon as the boys reached the age of sixteen arrangements were made for them to be employed as farm labourers. Only one was retained by the mission to do the jobs that the girls were unable to do, like driving the truck to collect the rubbish, emptying the toilet pans, delivering grapefruit from the orchard to the grapefruit shed, carting wood and driving the farm machinery.

In extreme times the girls' duties around the mission were extended to working on jobs out in the paddocks where extra hands were needed. In the hay-carting season skinny teenage girls like Doris and her schoolmates were expected to lift bales onto the back of the truck. By the end of the day their thin arms would be sore and covered in scratches.

One Saturday afternoon a bush fire was raging north-west of the mission and the hot summer winds were blowing it towards the dry stubble paddocks and threatening the mission community. The same group of teenagers were called out to assist. They were the ones who carried the buckets of water in pairs through the smoke to the firefighters, and kept their water tanks filled as they fought to contain the bush fire. The mission boys and girls had to run barefoot through the smoke and smouldering grass.

The mission wasn't a really bad place and there were moments when Doris appreciated being there. Like the evening when Matron Murray came into the common room and handed out pieces of paper and pencils and told them: "You can write to anyone you want to." Doris didn't have to think about the person that she wanted to write to — she wrote to her auntie Nancy Marshal who was still at the East Perth Girls' Home awaiting domestic work in the country somewhere. Back came an answer with instructions for Doris not to forget who her mother was. Recalling the information Gracie Toby had given her just before leaving Moore River, Doris sent the next letter to "Mrs Molly Craig, care of Baffa Danns Station".

Then one beautiful spring afternoon Matron handed Doris a letter, and because the mail was opened and censored she had no idea where it came from. Doris fought back the tears as she read the letter, her first letter from her own mother. Doris treasured that letter and when she was sad and feeling morose she took it out and read it in a quiet place by herself. This was the beginning of what was to become a regular and strong communication link between her and her mother. She had mixed feelings when a letter included photos of her family who had remained at Balfour Downs. She was ashamed to discover that her father was a Mardu or full-blooded black man. Doris certainly didn't want the rest of the girls knowing that fact. From the missionaries and other girls there were constant criticisms and condemnation of her full-blood relations, sowing suspicion and fear of the traditional Mardu cultural practices and belief systems. This drove a wedge between Doris and her people, and to protect herself from the hurtful taunts she hid the photos and letters under her pillow and only brought them out when she was alone.

Then one day, just before her first Christmas at Roelands, a very special letter arrived and it held money — there were two dust-covered, tobacco-stained ten shilling notes. Doris held the precious notes in her hand then Matron Murray rushed over with an empty jar and ordered her: "Put that foul-smelling, filthy money in this jar."

Doris liked the smell of tobacco and stood rubbing her fingers in the film of red dust on the notes. It reminded her of someone — yes, someone really special. She was overcome with nostalgia, she felt like crying, but didn't know why.

"I said you'll get them back when they have been laundered," said Matron so loudly that it jolted Doris back to the present.

She tried and tried for days after to understand what that special letter had released in her memory. She was haunted by it but sadly she just could not remember. It wasn't long after that incident that the missionaries began in earnest their campaign against the mission children's Aboriginal ties. These adults who conditioned and indoctrinated the Aboriginal children in their care were confident that the children would lose all memories of their actual families and thus their Aboriginal heritage.

Doris was confused when only negative aspects of her culture were used to create fear of Aboriginal culture and customs, but worst of all were the descriptions like "devil worshippers" and "primitive savages". The missionaries did not realise how soul-destroying and emotionally destructive those labels were and what devastating effect they had on Doris, who was a child at the time. They never had any idea of just how traumatic it would be for her in the future. The missionaries consciously or unconsciously were continuing the process of isolating Aboriginal children and alienating them from their own families and communities. The authorities worked to ensure that they had little or no contact with other Aboriginal people. Young people from the mission were placed in employment in areas where they had little chance of coming into contact with the local Aboriginal people.

* * *

One spring Sunday morning during Sunday morning service, an incident occurred that not only upset Doris, but helped her to do something that she had never done before: she made a decision that would change her life, her own decision.

Doris had become bored and uninterested in the sermon. Her gaze wandered to the green paddock and bright golden dandelions outside. As she refocussed her gaze to the other side of the room, her eyes met the smile of twelve-year-old Michael. Doris responded with a quick smile.

Matron noticed the friendly exchange between them and interpreted it in her own un-Christian, narrow-minded manner as something sordid and improper. After the service Doris was taken into Matron's kitchen and given a stern warning about "that kind of behaviour". She was so upset that she cried for some time. So while everyone was down at the river where a couple of baptisms were being performed, Doris decided to leave the mission. After all, she had reached the legal age of sixteen, she considered her options and made a decision to see Mr Cross as soon as the office opened the following morning.

She met with the superintendent and told him, "I want to leave the mission. But I don't want to work for any farmer's wife," she added firmly.

"Alright," his tone was calm. "What would you like to do?"

"I want to work in a country hospital as a wards maid," Doris said quietly.

"Well," he said, his mind ticking over as he pondered Doris's request. "I have just the thing for you." He showed her a brochure about a new course being introduced at the Royal Perth Hospital, a nursing aide training course that prepared a girl to work with the general nursing staff.

"Would you like to do that course?" he asked.

"Yes," came Doris's reply, without hesitation.

"Alright, but there's a catch," he began. "You'll have to go back to school to reach the education level required. What do you think about that? It would mean you will have to stay here and study for the next two years," he added, looking directly at her and waiting for her reply.

"Yes, I'm prepared to stay and work hard."

Doris completed the course with the Western Australian School of the Air by correspondence in two years. She sat for the Nursing Aide Entrance exam and passed, then submitted an application to the Royal Perth Hospital. Doris waited anxiously for the results. They came in the form a large brown envelope informing her that she was accepted into the course.

Doris would miss her friends, the long bush walks, standing outside watering the garden while listening to Ian Brown, the son of her favourite teacher, playing beautiful pieces on the piano. She would miss the annual holidays at Dunsborough campsite, swimming in the ocean and playing on the white sandy beaches — that was one holiday justifiably earned and enjoyed. Swimming in the pool down the river was never the same afterwards. There would be no more walking across the frost-covered playing fields in bare feet to prepare breakfast for the missionaries or to light the coppers and start the laundry or the ironing or whatever the day's tasks might be.

In April 1955 the day for her departure arrived, she packed her suitcase and said goodbye to her mission brothers and sisters. She sat in the back of Mr Cross's light blue Morris and shut the door. Before she left the dormitory she had placed the black leather-bounded Bible, a gift from Matron Murray on her sixteenth birthday, on her pillow and left it there.

This gift had become a tradition on the morning of a girl's sixteenth birthday, when she was given a beautiful Bible — which became something of a symbol. She had reached an important milestone in her life on the mission. Sixteen was the legal age that all girls could become domestic servants to any so-called Christian family who was willing to employ them.

As Mr Cross drove past the big noticeboard taking Doris through the gates of the Roelands Native Mission Farm for the last time, she made a promise to herself.

"I'm leaving this place for ever; I'm not coming back."

CHAPTER 10

Neon Lights and Romantic Nights

DORIS AND HER COUSIN MARGERY CONWAY ARRIVED at the Perth Central Railway Station where they were met by the parents of one of the missionaries at Roelands. The city was grey, dull and very noisy, and everyone seemed to be in a hurry, rushing around here and there. What a miserable lot of people. There were no greetings or smiles of acknowledgment.

After tea that evening the two girls were taken to the nurses quarters at the old Forrest Hotel in St George's Terrace which was to become Doris's new home. The next morning she met the rest of the student nursing aides in the dining room for breakfast. She was glad to see that there were four other Aboriginal girls among them. All except a girl named Laurel were from the country further south than the mission.

At dawn the next day she stood before the mirror, she was pleased with the image it reflected back. Standing there in the official lemon-coloured nursing aide uniform was the mission girl who had chosen to become a woman with a purpose. On that cool autumn morning in March 1955, Doris entered a new phase of her life. She was taking on an important responsibility as the first of the mission girls to qualify for a career that broke from the usual path of domestic labour. Others would follow her example because, like it or not, she was now a role model.

It didn't matter that her uniform was not blue — she was assured that she and the rest of the nursing aide students could expect the same respect and would have the opportunity to demonstrate the same skills as the other nurses once they were on the duty roster in the hospital. Each student was deep in thought as the driver of the Royal Perth Hospital bus travelled down his customary route to the hospital. This bus transported all the nursing staff to work for their shifts and back to the quarters, when they completed their shifts. The shuttle service began at 6.30 am and ended at 11.00 pm. The group were instructed to wait at a designated place at the hospital, where they were met by the tutors of the Nursing Aide Preliminary Training School, Sister Freeman and Staff Nurse James.

After a brief welcome the students were shown around the school which was situated near the medical students' flats. This tour was followed by a quick lesson in hospital protocol, such as students were to remain standing with their hands behind their backs when in the presence of senior members of the nursing staff and all medical personnel. There was a special reason for this advice — a few minutes later they were to meet with Matron Seagal, the head of all Nursing staff, and her deputy Sister Johnston, the head of the Nursing Aide Trainees Scheme.

The ten very nervous young women filed into the Matron's lounge room where they were congratulated on being successful applicants. The students realised that they were in the presence of two of the most powerful women in one of the largest teaching hospitals in the state. With that ceremony over, a tour of the hospital was most welcomed. It took care of the rest of the morning, up to lunchtime.

The Nursing Aide course was open to any applicant who, like Doris, didn't have the education level to be trained as a State Registered Nurse, or who had not reached the required age, which was eighteen years.

The afternoon session was devoted to learning about the hierarchical system that existed in both the nursing and the medical professions and the correct forms of address for hospital personnel. At nine the next morning their classes began with the daunting task of learning how to become a nursing aide.

Doris was aware from her school days that in order to succeed at lessons she must develop her own memorising abilities. Like other Aboriginal children she learned from the old people who had trained themselves to memorise quickly. Doris was determined to do the same.

The eight-week course was intense with theory in the mornings and practical experience in the afternoon. When the classes ended it was a relief to return to their quarters and relax. The course seemed to come to an abrupt end. "Be proud of your uniforms. You are now part of the hospital nursing team," Sister Freeman congratulated them. Their preliminary training completed, their names were included on the general roster. Doris was rostered on the same ward as her cousin Margery and she was very pleased about that.

At the end of her first week on duty Doris decided that she couldn't wish for a more friendly team of nurses — male and female — whom she could assist in small tasks in helping the patients through the healing process or, if there was no cure, making them as comfortable as she could.

While the preliminary school was in progress, Doris enjoyed having the weekends off. Half of the group spent the time with their families in the city, the others explored the city and investigated what was available in the way of recreation and entertainment. But during the first two weeks a great deal of time and energy was spent getting accustomed to the sounds and pace of the city.

Doris was content performing the simple duties on the wards of the hospital, but she was beginning to be mortified to find just how naive she was, that she was an unsophisticated eighteen-year-old woman who knew nothing about the facts of life. Often, when the off-duty nurses would gather and talk, Doris would display her mission upbringing in her lack of appreciation of subtle or suggestive jokes, particularly ones with sexual references. Even when she met a young Aboriginal man who had had a schoolboy crush on her at the Carrolup Settlement, she was pleased to see him.

One day she was waiting outside the cinema with her friend Lena, who'd left Moore River before Doris. A man called out to her, "Come here. I want to talk to you." Doris started towards him when her friend stopped her.

"He doesn't want to just talk to you, he wants to do rude things to you," Lena warned.

Doris wasn't sure what that meant, but she knew it meant something wrong and sinful. But it wasn't until she was on roster in Ward 2 that she first saw a naked man. Doris's awkwardness in this situation led to Sister Greenwood making a quick phone call, then instructing the young nursing aide to attend the nurses' lecture theatre that afternoon where she sat through a documentary about the human reproductive organs and their functions. From that she gained some scientific knowledge about conception, but nothing about the practical and emotional side of seduction and sexuality. This Doris had to learn by trial and error.

Living independently, away from the regulated mission life, was another aspect of life Doris would have to teach herself. Working as a nurse's aide meant long and varied shifts but she was able to balance her life between work and relaxation.

One day, when all the city's parks and gardens were filled with flowers Doris's friend Lena introduced her to a young white man. He was an apprentice diesel mechanic with the Western Australian Railways. He was also a musician, a flugelhorn player in a brass band. His name was Billy Stewart. Doris agreed to go with him to the movies.

On the way home he led her into the dark doorway of a shop where he kissed her gently at first and then with ardour. Then his hand slipped up her dress, touching her. She shoved his hand away roughly and ran back to the safety of her room. Doris took a long hot shower, desperate and confused, she tried to erase the shock of that experience.

The next day Lena rang to ask about her first date.

"It was alright," she told her friend.

"Are you going out with him again?"

"No," Doris answered quickly, "I don't like him."

"Why don't you like him, he's nice," said Lena.

"He's got dirty nails and smelly feet," Doris answered. But she never mentioned anything about his amorous desires. Billy Stewart tried again several times to get a date with her, but Doris rejected his offers and advances.

Doris enjoyed the summer nights sitting in the deck chairs in the open-air theatres in the metropolitan areas watching the movies. Swimming also occupied her time after she came off duty. One late afternoon she and her friend Lena — known to her fellow nurses as Sandy — decided to go to the beach before tea.

They called into the fish and chips shop to buy some chips. In the corner seated by himself was a handsome young soldier. He looked very familiar to Doris. Then she remembered, he was a patient whom she had nursed in Ward 2.

"Hello Danny," she greeted him cheerfully.

"Hello," he replied then invited them to have a cup of coffee with him. But when he stood up she realised that she had made a mistake. Although he had the same blonde, curly hair and blue eyes, this man was taller.

"You are Danny Hahn?" Doris asked him.

"My name is Danny, but my surname is Elden," he replied.

"Oh, I'm terribly sorry," she mumbled and began to walk away, most embarrassed.

"Don't go." He asked the two friends, "Where are you off to?"

"We're going for a swim."

"Wait and I'll come with you." So the three of them took a taxi to Swanbourne beach.

That afternoon swim was the beginning of a beautiful relationship. Lena was in the next intake of the Nursing Aide Training, so the two were able to plan days off together. When they weren't together dating or swimming, Doris and Lena joined their friends at the Coolabooroo League, an Aboriginal social club, where Doris loved to dance. The romance between Doris and Danny flourished, and developed into a strong and serious affair. All the themes of the current songs and films were about romance and being in love. Doris couldn't have wished for anything better, everything was perfect.

While he was still on leave Danny told her he had a surprise for her. It was a lovely Sunday morning and Doris rode along in the front seat of the Holden car borrowed from Danny's army friend. When they stopped outside a house in Kalamunda that had a beautiful front garden with a neat green lawn Danny announced, "Here we are."

"Who lives in this lovely house?" Doris asked, glancing quickly around the neat garden.

"You'll see," Danny told her, looking down at her with a big grin on his face.

Her love for this handsome blonde-haired six-foot soldier was beyond explanation, was something she had never imagined in her wildest dreams. She remembered their first kiss as they sat on the beach. Doris now wished it would go on forever.

The pair reached the door and when Danny knocked it

was opened by an attractive fair-headed lady who had a shocked look on her fine face.

"Mum, this is Dot," he said, still holding her small hand in his larger one. Mrs Elden shook the hand that was offered to her.

"Please come in," she said with a frosty smile on her face.

Danny's father was a huge man with the same features as his son and was much friendlier than his wife. His welcome was genuine. Dinner was roast lamb and all the trimmings, followed by a dessert of stewed fruit from their orchard with custard and cream. When the meal was over, while Danny and his father Alfred retired to the lounge with their beer and cigarettes, Doris assisted Mrs Elden with the washing up.

"I know you're a nice, educated girl, but I don't think my son is ready to marry yet," she said, looking sideways at Doris. "His father and I would like to see him become a career soldier." She added, "We want what is best for him."

Her meaning was clear, but not entirely honest. What Mrs Elden meant was that Doris was an Aboriginal girl who was her son's love, his girlfriend, but to be her daughter-in-law — that would not be accepted. Doris knew that Danny didn't have leadership qualities, he had no desire to become an officer. He was content to be a bombardier in the artillery corp.

Doris had no intention of giving him up just to please his mother. After all, Doris had been taking orders from white women all her life — from the day that she was born white people controlled and dominated her life. "For your own good," they said — but not this time, Doris decided. Meeting Danny Elden was the best thing that had happened to her so far and Doris hoped that it would remain that way for a long time.

The long hot summer days were almost over when a stranger came into their life and, to Doris, it was for the sole purpose of breaking up this perfect relationship. He was Danny's brother-in-law. He spread vicious rumours about Danny that drove Doris to write a very hurtful letter to Danny without first finding out the truth. She learned from her friend Lena that it was all instigated by Danny's mother. Hastily she sent another letter apologising profusely but all was in vain. Danny was enroute to Malaysia with his regiment.

His mother got her way in the end — Doris never saw Danny again.

Broken-hearted and traumatised by their breakup, Doris resigned from the hospital and moved to Perth's northern suburbs where she found employment in a nursing home, then later in a private hospital in Mt Hawthorn. She lost all interest in men generally, refusing to go on dates organised by her well-meaning friends, instead preferring the company of friends and fellow nurses.

Then one balmy summer's evening she met a Nyoongah man, a soldier who had just returned from service in Korea. He was thinking of re-enlisting for another six years in the army, but the slim dark curly-haired nurse helped him to change his mind. His name was Gerard Pilkington and he had all the qualities that she liked in a man, but most of all he loved her as equally as she loved him.

Doris left all the flashing neon lights, the romantic nights, the pace and noise of the city to live in Northam, a country town a couple of hour's drive east of Perth.

After the birth of their two daughters, first Bernadine then Geraldine, they decided to move to a rural town, Mukinbudin, to work on a farm. Doris never dreamed that this journey was going to be far more challenging than anything she had yet experienced in her life.

CHAPTER 11

The Move to Mukinbudin

D ORIS, HER HUSBAND GERRY and their two small daughters, Bernadine and Geraldine, arrived at their new home in the early hours on a freezing cold morning in June 1960. A blazing fire was hastily lit to provide warmth and light as she settled her two toddlers down for the rest of the night, then Doris slid into bed beside her husband and was soon fast asleep.

The next morning she had great difficulty containing her disappointment as she stood by the fire and surveyed the place that had been chosen as her new home. There were no shouts of joy or excitement, instead there was only disillusion and despair. The small sagging tent, pitched on a rich landowner's property, was a far cry from her visions of a small cottage with a garden of flowers, shrubs and trees.

For the past two years Doris and Gerry had lived with members of his family, so she saw the move from the city to Mukinbudin as an opportunity to fulfill a dream of having their own home where she could take good care of her family. Although she was warned about the ups and downs along life's highway and the hardships she was expected to endure, Doris was totally unprepared for the hardships as a farm labourer's wife and a mother living in a tin shack miles from the nearest neighbour.

Her husband Gerry tried to make his family as comfortable as he could. The first change he made was to erect the tent properly so that it didn't sag and Doris didn't have to crawl on her hands and knees any more. The tent became their bedroom. The kitchen was built from discarded iron found on the farm and there was space for a large fireplace and windows on the north and south sides of the kitchen, to let the light in and also to allow the smoke to escape. It wasn't what Doris had imagined or hoped for, but it provided her with privacy and a sense of ownership, most importantly, they were a family at last.

It was mid-winter and the rain had set in early, the wheat and other grains were sown. Gerry and his brother Bernie did all the maintenance work on the farm equipment. Ray Shadbolt, their employer, was one of the most influential and wealthy men, not only in Mukinbudin — a small community in the northern wheatbelt — but throughout the whole district. He had clout and just to mention his name got positive results for the families of his employees. For example, they received the best cuts of meat from the butcher.

The winter rains continued, forming puddles around the camp and turning the red clay earth into a quagmire, and filling the tent with water. But Doris did not let that bother her for she knew that seasons changed and situations improved. She just had to be patient and wait for spring to arrive. Doris made the effort to adjust to the rural surrounds and once that happened she concentrated on coping with camp living, at the same time raising her two daughters. It was frustrating without an older sister or another female relative to advise her.

All the chores had to be done without electricity, including the washing and ironing. Cooking meals in an open fireplace was less difficult to master. Doris had to learn to be patient and to accept failures; the important lesson learnt by trial and error was that she would eventually succeed. However, the tasks were often time-consuming and stressful. One day she tried to make a damper, a task which seemed quite easy — after all, Doris had observed the camp women at Moore River make scores of perfect dampers.

"It's nothing," they told her, "it's all in the wrist."

There shouldn't be any problems, she was going to make a lovely golden damper. She removed it from the hot ashes with great expectations and she was delighted with the sight of the golden round damper. It looked perfect, but when she broke it open, she was disappointed to discover that the inside was doughy and uncooked, a complete failure. Quickly she dug a hole near the huge marri tree and buried her failed attempt at making her first damper.

She felt a surge of panic rising inside her chest as she looked at the clock. Gerry was due home for lunch soon, so what was this failed cook going to do? Doris had to think of an alternative and quickly. Fortunately she had lots of flour left over so she hurriedly made pastry for a batch of pasties, but without an oven to bake them she had to fry them. Served with mashed potato, peas and carrots her meal was a success.

She forgot the botched damper and enjoyed her lunch, and so did her family.

From that day onwards Doris confidently improvised or planned meals around the kind of ingredients she had available in her cupboard.

The rain had ceased and the bitterly cold easterly winds that followed came to an end. It was lovely sitting in the sun enjoying the surroundings or taking her daughters for a walk, accompanied by her sister-in-law Rose and her three children. Those were enjoyable times.

Then one frosty cold night Doris went out to the toilet and as she squatted down behind a big marri gum tree she noticed something stark white on the ground near the large tree on her right, the place where she had buried the botched damper.

Doris became alarmed, "It's alive," she thought. "Dear Lord," she prayed silently as she walked towards the white spot, "Help me." Doris approached the spot and touched it gingerly with her slippered foot. It moved. She picked it up and held it in the glow of the hurricane lamp. It was just a piece of frost-covered bark from the tree. She almost burst out laughing, but stifled it, turning it into a cough. Climbing back in to bed she cuddled up behind the warm body of her husband, settled down and soon dozed off to sleep again.

No one mourned the passing of winter, but everyone celebrated the arrival of spring. Fields and paddocks burst into carpets of bright wildflowers. The idyllic scenery compensated for the lack of modern comforts such as electricity and running water. Doris even got used to sleeping on the homemade bed constructed by her husband. Their humble tent home was filled with peace and happiness and improvements were made every week. All around them the landscape was full of beauty and splendour. Every morning as Doris rose to greet a new day she silently paid tribute to the Creator for providing the magnificence of yet another spring. Every day was better than the one before.

Then one day a small cream-coloured Prefect pulled up in the clearing near their camp. Rose and Doris had been sitting outside in the warm sunshine having morning tea.

"Who's that?" inquired Rose rather loudly.

"I don't know. I can't see from here," Doris replied as she strained to identify the occupants of the car. But as soon as she did recognise them, Doris froze. It was Mum, Pop Calvin and Paul, Gerry's mother, stepfather and brother.

"Oh no," said Rose. "Come on, Sis, we better go up and meet them." Doris knew the instant her in-laws pitched their tent her peaceful existence was doomed.

"Dear Lord," she prayed, "I don't mean to be unkind, but you know that I've been roughing it, making the best with what we have and I have done fairly well so far, but I don't think that I could cope with my mother-in-law." Even before she settled in, her domineering and insensitive attitude that had caused so much pain and anxiety in the past was set in motion. Her presence seemed to bring out the negative side of her son's personality. The criticism, the sarcasm and humiliation heaped on Doris were made worse by her husband's change of attitude. Doris felt abandoned and neglected. Then she discovered that she was pregnant again.

Doris, this meek woman whose downfall was her Christian upbringing, became a victim to her mother-in-law. "Respect your elders", Doris was instructed by her teachers. So she allowed this woman to abuse and humiliate her. She had never responded harshly to any Aboriginal adult in her life, and besides, she had never met a woman like her mother-in-law before.

She made it quite clear that Doris was an unsuitable wife for her son for the simple reason that her family did not come under the Native Act and Doris did. Doris felt alienated and uncomfortable. Her husband's family were categorised as being "octoroons", one-eighth Aboriginal.

The pace quickened on the farms as harvesting time came around. Large trucks were thundering along the roads delivering grain to the wheat silos to be stored ready to be transported by goods train to the grain terminal at Fremantle in the south-west. This was the busiest and most important summertime event on the wheat growers' calendar. Gerry's family became used to seeing him come home covered in grain dust. Soon the harvesting ended without any mishaps and the farmers and their labourers were able to rest, some went for holidays down to the city or other coastal towns.

All the family had Christmas dinner at Popes Hill, the home of Gerry's cousin Willy and his family. During the Christmas holidays Gerry stayed on at the farm to take care of the farm animals while the boss and his family went south for a holiday. Doris's mother-in-law, Pop and Paul moved over to another farm on the far side of the farm from where Doris and Gerry lived. Rosie and Bernie and their family returned to Perth for the Christmas holidays. Peace returned to their selection.

* * *

One extremely hot summer day Doris and her daughters were sitting under the shade of a tea-tree in a sandy creek bed when she saw something that she had never seen before. It looked like rain, but as it approached across the stubble fields she realised that it was definitely not rain, but something more frightening. It was a cloud of thick, red-brown dust.

She and her daughters fled to the safety of their tent. The pregnant mum rushed around securing the guy ropes of the tent, fastening the windows and doors. Doris stepped outside to check on the position of the dust storm and saw that it was almost upon them. She settled down with her children to sleep it out.

An hour later she awakened to find the dust storm had passed leaving red-brown dust so thick that it weighed down the tent. The dust storm was followed by heavy showers of rain. Doris liked the smell of the rain in summer and loved to watch the clouds roll above her, scattering showers of cool clear rain drops. Once she got used to the slushy mud between her toes it wasn't so bad.

Day by day, as her pregnancy advanced, Doris experienced extreme tiredness as well as discontentment. She began to think that she and her family should be living under better conditions than these. No one understood that she had not been trained in raising babies. She was totally unprepared and needed someone to guide her.

Requests were made regularly to the boss to build a small cottage on the property somewhere. It wasn't that he couldn't afford to build one — he was, after all, one of the richest farmers in the district. The answer was always the same — "soon". Enduring the loneliness and the desire for other women's company, and other needs not being met, Doris blundered along, learning exactly what was involved in being a mother of two girls living in isolation.

Meanwhile the constant criticism, the sarcasm and intimidation continued. Some days were worse than others. The darkness of depression was building up around her and Doris seemed to attract all the negative energy that emerged from that dark well. Those days were filled with anxiety, but the fears were often overcome by the company and love of her children. They brought love and joy to her very sad existence, and her faith in the Lord prevented her from having a nervous breakdown.

Continued pressure for better living conditions for her family was top priority. These requests were made weekly until her husband Gerry plucked up enough courage to ask the boss again.

"When are we going to build that cottage for my family?"

"Soon," the boss replied.

"How soon?" asked Gerry. That question was never answered, nor was the promise kept.

With no prospect of a decent home to raise her children Doris became even more anxious and depressed. She thought hard and long about taking medication to control her mood. She had seen how other women suffered from the side effects — that put her off completely. No, she told herself, pills were not the answer, but music was.

Doris decided to control her depression and loneliness by turning the knob on her radio. After that the oblong-shaped object with a cheesecloth covering became her constant companion. It kept her informed and entertained, but most of all this prized possession prevented her from falling into the dark abyss of insanity. Her precious radio became the symbol of inner peace and sanity.

One picturesque spring afternoon, while Doris sat near the dam in the corner of a paddock doing the washing, every now and then she would pause to take in the landscape which was emblazoned once again with colour. Spring, she sighed, is the time for love. Bernadine and Geraldine, played happily nearby. The radio was playing softly. It was good to be alive. The radio presenter announced the next recording. Doris stopped washing. She listened so intently with both her heart and ears that she appeared to be frozen.

> I dreamed I dwelt in marbled halls,
> with vassals and serfs at my side,
> and of all who assembled within those walls
> that I was the hope and the pride,
> I had riches too great to count,
> could boast of a high ancestral name.

She gazed across the field of golden dandelions, and allowed herself to be carried on the wings of song. The voice of Joan Sutherland soared beyond reality. Doris closed her eyes and saw an image of herself as she was three years ago. There was a slender, dark-haired woman in a pale blue chiffon gown descending the white and gold staircase. She was smiling at all present in the hall below.

> … but I also dreamt which pleased me most,
> That you loved me still the same,
> That you loved me still the same.
> I dreamt that suitors sought my hand,

That knights upon bended knee,
and with vows no maiden heart could withstand,
They pledge their faith to me.

The young woman stepped down from the last step into the hall.

And I dreamt that one of that noble host
came forth my hand to claim.

All her friends were among the guests. Doris was their role model, their leader. The vision so wonderful that she wished that it would stay there for a while longer. She was completely overcome by the power and emotion of that beautiful song from *The Bohemian Girl*, by Balfe and Bunn.

She opened her eyes and lowered her head to see a very pregnant body that was bursting the seams of her faded black and pink shift, last year's Christmas present from her husband. What would her friends say and think if they saw her now? They would be wondering what happened to the fit, smartly dressed young woman they once knew and respected. She had changed into someone who had gone from seven and a half stone to eleven stone through comfort eating. Tears filled her eyes and spilled down her cheeks. Her knees were covered with dirty soap suds. Doris wiped her eyes on the sleeve of her shift and continued listening to the radio and washing the clothes by hand. She was brought back to harsh reality instantly when her daughters called out excitedly. "Daddy! Daddy!" The radio was switched off quickly and covered with a towel.

"What, haven't you finished yet?" asked her husband.

"No, not yet," she replied meekly. Gerry picked up the two

four-gallon drums of water and carried them back to their camp. Doris was glad because, when he was at work, she had to cart her own water.

She watched as her husband approached the fence, climbed over it and walked military style along the narrow path that led to their camp. Their daughters chatted happily beside him. When they were out of sight Doris switched the radio back on just in time to hear the end of the song. She had discovered earlier in their relationship that Gerry hated classical music. This naive young woman assumed that everyone enjoyed listening to Mozart, Beethoven, Chopin and other great European composers, but she was sadly mistaken. He made comments like: "What are you listening to that s … t for?", or he referred to it as "high brow" or "long-haired stuff". Doris was deeply offended by those negative remarks. It was then that she decided to revert to more cunning and deceitful methods so that she could enjoy her music in secret and at the same time preserve her sanity.

Her two little girls were asked never to tell their father about the radio. It was their secret. Doris scrimped and saved to buy batteries, and when the radio's wires became loose or broken she waited until Gerry went to work before she soldered them back together again. Doris worked hard to keep her radio in good working order. It was her elixir of life.

Gerry wasn't a bad person, despite the humiliation and intimidation he inflicted on her in the presence of others. But she knew that when they were alone in their canvas tent at night he became the loving, caring man that she loved.

> … but I also dreamt which charmed me most,
> that you loved me still the same,

that you loved me still the same,
that you loved me, you loved me the same.

With the washing done and hung out on the fence to dry, Doris waddled along the narrow path to her home and family. This was reality, a rural life of hardship, toil and tears. How can any woman be enthusiastic about this?

* * *

Doris blundered along making discoveries and learning through trial and error. Then one hot summer's day help and support came from an unexpected source. She was sitting on a bench outside Sirr's General Store when two little Aboriginal girls approached her and asked her, "Are you Doris?"

"Yes I am," she replied.

"Well," said the blonde-haired one, "Mum said would you like to come to our place to have a cup of tea?"

"Thank you very much, I'd love to," she told the girls. "I'll follow you," she said happily as she put her two daughters in the strong, old cane pram.

"What are your names?" Doris asked them.

Quick as a flash came a cheery reply, "My name is Gloria and this is my sister Celia."

That invitation was the most welcomed words that she had heard since arriving in Mukinbudin. In fact this was her first taste of country hospitality, one that she would remember always. This small gesture developed into a firm and lasting friendship with the girl's parents, Blanche and Hughie Headland, who had the largest family in town — nine children, six girls and three boys. Blanche became Doris's mentor and friend, who supported her and guided her through the stages of motherhood. Consequently she became a more confident and capable young mother, but it was just as pleasing to know that she and her small family became part of the Headland's larger one.

Christmas Day celebrations were a highlight that year, because of sharing the festivities with the Headland family. It was an absolutely happy day, with good food, good cheer and a wonderful atmosphere of well-being. The New Year brought renewed hope for the new home where Doris could show off her culinary and homemaking skills. She would show her critics that she was the most suitable wife for a soldier who had served overseas in Korea. As a mother Doris improved greatly and developed skills that she never thought she could. She made a colourful patchwork quilt using materials from cast-off clothing to beautify her tent home.

There was still no sign of the new cottage, but the birth of her first son brought joy to their humble home. That lovely little boy, named Sonny, became everybody's baby.

* * *

The year 1961 brought changes that were to affect the whole family. Pop Calvin was able to negotiate and set up a small business for himself and his sons as contract workers, doing jobs such as fencing, clearing paddocks of stones, and root picking. This was certainly good news because this meant that their income would be increased. So for a while the atmosphere of the camp improved. There was a feeling of contentment and hope for the future.

Then one day there was a dispute over wages. The sons, Gerry and Bernie, expected a three-way split, but they were told by their stepfather that they were subcontractors and therefore were not entitled to an equal share of payment received. The contracting business was terminated, Pop and Bernie accepted work as farm labourers while Gerry returned to work for Ray Shadbolt.

One day Gerry came home from work and announced that he had found a better campsite and that he had building materials for a bigger and better home. It was certainly a much better location, close to the windmill and tank of clear fresh water, shaded by large wattle trees with clean white sand for the children to play on. Doris wasn't sad to see the tent bedroom being dismantled and taken to the rubbish tip. The iron and timber-framed shack was a big improvement on their first camp. This one-bedroom house was large enough to accommodate a large double bed, two single beds, and a cot for Sonny. Doris and her family settled in quite happily.

In July the following year another daughter was born. She was named Michele, and she had the bluest eyes her mother Doris ever saw. Her family was complete.

About that time Bernie and Rose and their children decided to move back to Perth, and Doris missed their company and support. The two families had formed a strong bond. Shortly after, Pop and Mum Calvin and Paul pulled up outside their shack, the little cream Prefect loaded with their belongings. They were moving to Geraldton to be with Pat Leigh and Pauline Howard, Gerry's sisters, and their families. Their departure brought complete happiness and contentment to Doris and her family and peace dwelt in their humble dwelling on the edge of the north-west paddock.

The nervousness and the anguish vanished. Doris was able to relax and enjoy life. At night there was singing around the campfire as the children sat, all eyes fixed on their father while he sang the lovely Irish ballads like: "I'll Take You Home Again Kathleen" and "I Wandered Today on the Hills, Maggie". Doris was in paradise.

When spring came it seemed like all the flowers were blooming just for Doris and her family. The vows of love for Gerry her husband were renewed that spring. The panoramic view from their humble home was one of splendour. She enjoyed the harmonious relationship that existed between her family and nature.

Doris continued her weekly visits to her friends Blanche and Hughie and their children, sometimes staying overnight, but the weekends were reserved for family outings. Hunting was a favourite pastime for Gerry and Doris, and the children looked forward to these trips in the bush. Gerry made sure that the kerosene fridge was always filled with bush tucker. While her husband hunted the local game Doris and her four children explored the surrounding bushland.

One day they located an ideal picnic place under some shady she-oak trees. Clearing the pine-needle-like leaves Doris threw some blankets down on the clean white sand and they settled down to wait for the hunter to return. A gentle breeze began to blow through the leaves that hung limply on the clump of she-oak trees. A feeling of melancholy pervaded the space and Doris was overcome with nostalgia. Something tragic had occurred here.

Perhaps a woman had lost a husband or a child and a grieving spirit still remained at this place. Whatever had happened, there was a feeling of so much pain and suffering that Doris was moved to tears and the strange thing was that she had no idea why, but she felt like crying.

The settled routine of work and leisure never changed, so this enabled Doris to plan her own duties accordingly. As a result those days of unity and harmony were the happiest times. Then one day that all changed.

Doris noticed that Gerry's attitude was changing, becoming more negative towards her. She had experienced his mood swings before and had adjusted accordingly, but this time the negativity persisted longer than usual. She was upset and greatly disturbed when she learned that she had a rival for her husband's affections. He was the man of her dreams. What has she done to deserve this kind of treatment, she wondered, it didn't seem fair. She was taught that coveting another woman's husband was a sin. The Ten Commandments tells us in Exodus 20, verse 17: "Thou shalt not covet thy neighbour's wife."

Once more the bad dreams returned to haunt her. If he deserted her and abandoned his family, where could they go to seek refuge and comfort? Doris stood at the door of her shack and tried desperately to consider her options. There were little or no prospects. Her thoughts were interrupted by the rumble of thunder on the distant horizon. She raised her head slowly and focused her eyes on the approaching thunderstorm and there, in the grey sky above, was the brightest, certainly the most beautiful rainbow she had seen in a long while.

The words of a hymn that was often sung at the mission church services came to mind — it always gave her hope and

courage and she certainly needed that right now. Doris sang
in her heart,

> Oh joy that seekest me through pain,
> I cannot close my heart to thee,
> I trace the rainbow through the rain
> And feel the promise is not vain
> That morn shall tearless be.

As she wiped the tears from her eyes with the back of her
hand, a little voice called out. "Mummy, I'm hungry." Her
daughter Geraldine brought her back to reality. Her four
adorable children were the most precious gifts; no one would
take them away from her.

When the children were bathed and fed, they sat around
the fire to wait for their Dad to come home from work. Doris
was determined to suffer in silence and prayed to the Lord
for strength and guidance, and deliverance from this impossible situation. Some weeks later her prayers were answered.

It was a few months before Christmas 1962 when Gerry
announced that they would all be leaving Mukinbudin to
join Bernie and Rosie in Perth. Doris could hardly contain
her excitement. "Thank you, Lord" she said silently "for
finding a way of escape from this place." However, Doris
would miss her friends Blanche and Hughie, whose friendship and support she would always be grateful for.

On the morning of their departure Doris stood outside
the tin shack that had been the family home for the past year.
She gazed across the dry land that had been lush green
pastures for grazing animals, and wondered whether the
struggle and heartache she had endured recently would

cease. Would contentment be rediscovered? she asked herself.

She said her silent goodbyes to the fields of dry stubble, patches of earth and the beautiful mallee landscape of the wheatbelt. At that moment she felt as empty as the lifeless land itself, but unlike her the soil was sown with seeds, it had the certainty of revival — life would sprout after the first rains. There would be verdant pastures, grains and flowers would bloom again.

She refused to accept defeat. She was a fighter and that fighting spirit had manifested itself at her premature birth. But most of all, she had hope, the very substance of life itself and where there is hope, there will always be life and love.

The move back to the city would bring positive changes for Doris and her family. That was her hope and prayer.

* * *

Compared to the town of Mukinbudin, the city was paradise with plenty of fruit and fresh vegetables and lots of pleasant visitors. Doris had the opportunity to meet most of her husband's family, and his grandparents, Mary and Lewis Calgaret, became very special to her. She looked forward to visiting them every Sunday. She loved to listen to the stories of the early days at Guildford.

When Granny Lewis passed away, his wife Granny Mary — her mother-in-law's mother — died shortly after. Their deaths had a profound effect on Doris, who loved the old couple as deeply as her own kin. She had never seen her mother-in-law so heartbroken as she was on the day of Granny Mary's funeral.

"I've just lost my mother," she said to the tearful Doris, "you must go and look for yours."

As Doris shed more tears over the grave of one of her favourite women, she made a resolution to begin her search the next morning. She had last heard from her mother about seven years ago, just before she left Roelands. Doris hastily wrote a letter the following day and a few weeks later she received a letter from her parents. They were delighted to hear from their elder daughter and would be happy to spend Christmas with Doris and her four children, their grandchildren whom they had never seen.

So on 23 December 1962 Doris and her family left Perth to begin the most important journey of her life.

CHAPTER 12

Red Dust and Strong Tobacco

IT WAS ON CHRISTMAS EVE that Doris began that important journey to meet again with her mother and father whom she had not seen for more than twenty years. After settling Doris and the children comfortably in the cool carriage, Gerry stood waving until the train was out of sight. From the window of the railway carriage Doris saw a different kind of landscape from that she had known and lived in during the past few years. As the train twisted and turned through the dry red countryside of the Murchison region of Western Australia she watched with fascination the continual changes of scenery.

"Mummy, I want to go to the toilet," Geraldine's voice broke in.

"Me too," chorused Bernadine and Sonny.

Doris picked up baby Michele who was asleep on the seat beside her and took them all to the toilet. She then gave them a wash with cold water and told them to rest until the train reached Yalgoo, where all passengers alighted for refreshments.

Doris dozed, while her four children rested peacefully on the bunks. She had no recollection of the fateful train journey that she had taken as a toddler with her mother Molly and baby sister Anna in September 1941. But she would certainly remember this special trip because she was returning as a woman and a mother of four children — to her, the most precious gifts she ever received.

At the Yalgoo railway station Doris and her children sat outside on a bench to have their sandwiches and lemonade. She chatted to a young Yamatji man who informed her that they were halfway there. Refreshed, Doris and her family returned to their railway compartment and prepared for the remainder of the trip. It was an effort to control her anxiety, but she knew she couldn't help being apprehensive at meeting her parents from whom she had been separated for over twenty years.

She focused instead on the view of arid landscape and wide open plains that stretched for miles with few signs of habitation. Soon dusk was creeping across the countryside.

Doris bathed and dressed the children in their pyjamas, and settled them in their bunks. While they slept she listened to the clickety-click of the old steam train as it trundled westward through the warm summer night. The further it went the more regular and pronounced the sound became. It seemed to blot out all other sound, so all Doris could hear was the clickety-clack, clack, clickety-clack, clack of the wheels until, finally, she fell asleep too.

* * *

She was awakened by a knock on the door of the carriage. It was the young Yamatji man, Lance Mongoo.

"We're here now, at Meekatharra," he announced. "When you're ready, I'll give you a lift to your Auntie Carrie's house," he told Doris.

The sleepy children were arranged alongside their mother in the taxi, and Lance gave directions to the driver. The taxi stopped in front of a khaki-green steel house. "What is this place?" she asked Lance.

"This is the reserve. And that's old Carrie's house."

Lance helped Doris with her luggage, then departed, leaving her and her children in this God-forsaken place. Her first impression, after the green paddocks of the south-west, was of a dry desolate town, a place where a person would've had to have been born and bred to actually want to live. There were no trees; it looked an impossible place to settle down in.

Leaving the children to wait beside the luggage, Doris walked up to the door, knocked nervously and waited. A few moments later the door was opened to reveal an ancient Aboriginal woman, the only kin whose name Doris could remember. Her facial features didn't seem to have changed, she just looked older.

"Auntie Carrie, I'm Doris, Molly's daughter."

"Your mother is camping at that last house," she informed Doris, pointing down to the bottom of the reserve. "You'll know her, she's the only half-caste woman there."

With baby Michele on her hip Doris lifted the large suitcase and turned onto the gravel road leading towards her sleeping parents, when the old lady called out: "I'm not your auntie, I'm your granny." Doris was surprised, she hadn't realised she was related to the old lady. Carrie was her grandmother Maude's sister, her mother's aunt, and therefore Doris's grandmother in the Mardu kinship system.

As Doris led her son and two daughters to meet their grandparents, Molly and Toby, she glanced towards the eastern skies. A new day was dawning. Today was Christmas Eve, tomorrow would be Christmas.

The gold and pinkish hues of sunrise meant that, predictably enough, another scorching day was at hand. It seemed that the heat of the summer day began at dawn, or perhaps it was still the heat of yesterday that hadn't had time to cool down. In a couple of moments she would be reunited with two of the most important people in her life, Molly and Toby Kelly (Burungu).

The crunching of their shoes on the gravel road wakened the sleeping dogs who began barking and snarling at the new arrivals.

"Shut up you mongrels," shouted a deep-voiced man annoyed at being disturbed at this early hour.

Even though it was not yet day the heat was oppressive. To escape it everyone slept on makeshift beds outside their houses. As she approached Doris placed her suitcase near the sleeping form of the fairest woman in the group. She approached the woman and touched her lightly on the shoulder. The woman opened her eyes and focused them on her daughter.

"Hello," said Doris her voice filled with trepidation. "Do you know me?"

"No," came the reply and, without any hesitation or interest, Molly rolled over and went back to sleep.

The lump in Doris's throat made it difficult to swallow, but she regained her composure and tried once more. Her heart was filled with deep emotion. Fearing rejection, she repeated the question in the same words: "Do you know me?"

Her mother didn't answer, but this time her eyes focused on the four little ones seated on the large suitcase. Slowly raising herself on one arm, she called out excitedly, "My grandchildren! My daughter is here." Then she began to wail. The hot easterly winds carried the sound of a mother's cry to tell everyone that her daughter who was taken away as a child had returned as a woman and a mother. Other relatives came over and joined her.

"Why are these people crying, Mummy?" asked one of the little ones. "Who passed away?" The visitors were confused.

Doris learned later that this was a traditional custom practiced by her people as a way of expressing their feelings. They cry when someone dies, when they say goodbye, or for those who have died in their absence. But this morning Doris's mother and her relations were crying because she had been away for a long time and had now returned to her country and her people.

While her mother rushed about cooking breakfast of fried kangaroo and hot damper, Doris was able to get a better view of the surroundings. The conditions her parents lived in were a disappointment. It was basic and plain, and she hated to think of what her husband's reaction would be if he saw what his children were being exposed to. He and his family would have a fit. They were prejudiced against her people already, with Doris's mother-in-law forever reminding her that: "We don't come under the Native Act," and acting superior to the black-skinned people of the north-west and the eastern goldfields regions of the state.

Doris shuddered as she counted the numbers of mangy dogs that had attached themselves to the people who lived on that stony, treeless, government-allocated land. Not only did she and the children have to contend with the reserve dogs, the dust and flies, but as the sun rose higher they had the difficulty of getting used to the unbearable heat that beat down on the community. And there was the big disappointment that Doris's father, Toby, wasn't here to meet her. He was away on Law Business and would not return until the ceremonies were completed.

So Doris would have to bear these conditions for a couple of weeks longer if she wanted to meet him. Two weeks would definitely be the limit, she decided. The rest of the day was spent trying to keep cool in this treeless place.

The next day was Christmas Day and she thought this must be the most desolate, God-forsaken location in Western Australia to celebrate one of the most significant days in the Christian calendar. Where was the Christmas spirit and the Christmas cheer? There was nothing, no indication that it was Christmas, not even the exchange of wishes for "a merry Christmas". Her tears fell as she thought of other Australians who would be attending church services and spreading words of hope for peace on earth and goodwill to all mankind. "What sort of Christmas dinner will my children have?" she wondered.

Her anxiety disappeared when Auntie Daisy and her husband Uncle Scotty Tulloch and cousin June arrived home laden with Christmas dinner to share with Molly, Doris and the children. The Tullochs generously offered them better accommodation as well.

Setting the table was a great pleasure for June and Doris, the decorations were simple, but very effective. Everyone sat down to a Christmas dinner of cold chicken, baked potatoes, baked pumpkin, peas and salad, followed by Christmas pudding and custard, lollies, nuts and cool drinks. This special meal was shared with Molly. This was the best Christmas dinner in the outback and it was with joy that Doris wished all present "a very merry Christmas!"

* * *

The following weeks on the reserve were spent adjusting to the climate and becoming accustomed to the impoverished living conditions. Doris came to realise that she must humble herself, and settled down to learn something about her traditional history and culture. That required patience.

She was pleased to find herself a member of such a strong family unit. The rest of the visit was filled with activities such as outings in the bush, and cooking traditional foods in the traditional way directly in the hot embers, and eating hot damper dripping with butter and jam washed down with the milky sweet tea of her childhood memory. All through the Upper Murchinson and the Pilbara everyone has a sleep after their midday meal and starts moving around again in the late afternoon. One afternoon Doris and her four children were aroused from sleep by the women from her mother's camp.

"Doris, your Daddy's here, come and meet him."

"Hurry up," they called.

"Quick, Grandpop is here," Doris cried, urging her family

to move as fast as their little legs could carry them. She gathered Michele in her arms and rushed up to Molly's to wait for her father to arrive. The white Ford pulled up near the house. Molly guided her daughter towards it as the men piled out. She introduced them one by one as they approached her.

"This is Uncle Bob. This is your brother Patrick. This is your Uncle Joe. This is your Uncle Bert."

After each man shook hands with Doris he sat down in the shade of the house. There was one man left. He walked slowly towards Doris and she didn't need any introduction. She could feel the emotion that this humble man projected.

"This is your Daddy," said her mother tenderly.

Doris put her arm around his waist as she held her baby daughter, and rested her head on his shoulder. As he wrapped his arm around the young mother and child, his hand brushed the hair from Doris's cheek. His fingers traced her brow, stopping at the indentation, the identifying mark, made so many years ago in the attack by the cattle dog at Balfour Downs. His child, Nugi, had come home.

Overcome with emotion, her tears flowed freely. This Aboriginal man, going bald on the crown, his curly black hair sprinkled with grey, his clothes covered in red dust and smelling of strong tobacco — this was the person who sent her those two ten-shilling notes when she was a twelve-year-old schoolgirl in the mission. As his warm tears dropped onto her head she knew her Dad was a very special man. This was her beloved father whom the Commissioner for Aboriginal Affairs referred to as "the native from the desert".

He hugged his grandchildren as he held them in his arms

and everyone watching was moved to tears. They were witness to a memorable occasion for this father and his long-lost daughter whom he had not seen for over two decades. Throughout her life Doris had had substitute mothers but only one father and, right now, he was there with her.

Doris spent the next two weeks with her parents. Her heart swelled with pride each time she uttered those priceless words, "my Mum" and "my Dad". She dreaded having to be separated from them again. She realised that the nervousness she had experienced when she arrived was being replaced by a sense of sadness and uncertainty at the thought of saying goodbye. To her parents the parting meant a disruption to their happy reunion, and further heartache.

But Doris and her parents were determined not to let this parting end in grief. They made a silent vow to keep on being a family, even if they were to be parted. So two days before Doris and her small family were due to return to Geraldton, her mother Molly made a heart-rending request. She asked Doris if she would leave Sonny with them for a little while.

This was so unexpected that Doris was speechless. "I don't know what to say, let me think about it," she said finally.

"Your Daddy want to show him to the family," her mother added.

It was one of the most difficult decisions Doris had to make. From her father's point of view it seemed a reasonable request, but for Doris it created confusion and perplexity. Her only son was his father's pride and joy. He was also her Dad's first grandson. It seemed that the simple request wasn't so simple or easy to fulfill. Reluctantly, Doris allowed herself to be persuaded by her parents to leave her son with them.

She believed their request served a dual purpose for them. One was the opportunity for them to show off their first grandson to the rest of the relatives and the other reason, equally important, was to ensure that their recently returned daughter would definitely have to come back to collect her son.

On their return to Geraldton, Doris and her three daughters were warmly welcomed by Gerry, but when he noticed that his precious son was missing he became very angry.

He asked where Sonny was. Doris hesitated, but before she could answer, Bernadine and Geraldine happily told their father, "He's back there with Nanna and Pop."

Gerry swore, the delight that moments before was spread over his face turned instantly to disbelief and anger. What in God's name was she thinking about, leaving his pride and joy with "black, tribal people," he asked, forgetting they were her own flesh and blood. Doris had suffered from his hurtful remarks on a regular basis and she should have been used to them by now, but nonetheless, they still upset her. Later she had to contend with more disparaging comments from his mother.

Gerry ordered her to go back and bring Sonny home. But he soon realised that was impossible because Bernadine would be starting school that year so Sonny would have to stay with his grandparents until the school holidays in May. Doris waited anxiously for the first school term to end and when it did, she and her three daughters boarded the railway bus for Meekatharra. When they arrived she learned that her parents were at Turree Creek Station, working with the mustering team.

The next day Doris and her family hitched a ride to Turree Creek with some cousins and their boss from a neighbouring station. On reaching Terrace Creek they met Tom Hammond, the dogger, who explained that he was on his way to join the muster but volunteered to stay another night at the homestead. "That's your Mum and Dad's place over there," he told them, pointing to the large shed on the other side of the garden.

Doris thanked him and with baby Michele on her hip she lugged her cases to the shed. It was large and roomy but very dusty, so she got busy and swept and hosed the floor, then made the beds. There was a shower and laundry outside where the four refreshed themselves, then rested until late afternoon.

As the sun was setting beyond the gibber plains Tom Hammond brought them a bowl of stew, a large piece of damper and some boiled pudding and custard. This station meal was most appreciated by Doris and the girls. He left very early the next morning, leaving Doris and her three daughters alone at Turree Creek Station until the boss, Johnny Miller, and his Aboriginal station workers returned.

When the mustering team rode in and saw the washing on the clothes line they were curious. Doris's parents were very pleased to see their daughter but were saddened when she told them that Gerry insisted she take Sonny home to Geraldton.

After a few days break the team, and Doris and her children, returned to the mustering camp to complete the culling and branding, and the trucking of the cattle to the saleyards in Midland near Perth. Life at the mustering camp was interesting. The men and women rose at daybreak and finished work at sunset. Doris and her children looked forward to a cool wash at the tank after tea at night.

After the evening meal, while the Aboriginal men played cards at the single men's camp, the women sat in a small group apart from the main camp. The camp for the non-Aboriginal men was separate from their Aboriginal co-workers.

The days passed by so quickly that soon it was time to go home. This holiday was the beginning of many more, although that was the first and the last one to Turree Creek Station. During the Christmas break in 1963 Molly and Toby moved to the next station, Bulloo Downs.

Over the next ten years Doris and her family — including Gerry — would spend many happy days at Bulloo Downs learning about traditional foods and trying to memorise the traditional names of the animals and plants of the region. Those times were wonderful, times full of learning.

Molly and Toby lavished all their love and attention on their grandchildren. It didn't make up for all the years that they were deprived of being loving parents to their two daughters or compensate for their great loss, but it did help them realise that they were more fortunate than many others who had never had the opportunity to be reunited with their lost children.

CHAPTER 13

Waves of Discontentment

Geraldton was the ideal place to raise a family and settle down. Gerry and Doris agreed that it was the best move they had ever made. They found a place to rent; it was a one-bedroom cottage surrounded by a large beautiful garden — Doris's first dream home.

By now there were not one, but two, additions to the family — two more sons, named Gerard and Ricky. That made six — three boys and three girls. Now their family was complete. Gerry found employment with the Shire Council, working with the rubbish disposal unit. Peace and contentment reigned.

Then one day the owner of the property announced that he had a buyer for the place and they must vacate the premises in a few weeks time. When her mother-in-law heard about the latest development, she invited the family to come and stay with them. Doris shuddered at the thought of sharing a house with her.

For the next couple of weeks, when the two older girls left for school Doris would pile the four little ones into the large cane pram and walk up and down the gravel roads and streets searching for another home for her family. She would arrive home tired and disappointed. There seemed to be no empty houses available in the neighbourhood, so she and her husband decided to widen their search to the outlying districts.

Every afternoon after school the family drove up and down the dusty roads, all eyes looking out for what seemed like a deserted house. For days they would return home at dusk without finding anything. Then late one afternoon Doris spied a small house off the Nanson road in Waggrakine, at closer inspection they could see it was a dilapidated old house on a few acres of farm land.

The owner was uncertain whether he should be letting a house that had been condemned by the Shire, although Gerry offered to renovate the place at no cost to him.

Finally it was agreed that Gerry and his family could rent quite cheaply if Gerry would agree to be a caretaker for the owner's small flock of sheep that grazed in the nearby paddock. The move to Waggrakine proved to be the right one.

As Gerry earned no more than the basic wage, Doris was forced to buy the cheapest cuts of meat and experiment in ways of preparing wholesome meals for her family. Times were tough, but they seemed to manage quite well on a tight budget. Conditions improved a great deal after the vegetable garden began producing. Living there was like having their own farm. The sheep grazed contentedly in the fields, the chooks provided them with eggs and meat, and the ducks provided eggs for baking on Sundays, which was the day for the family outing. They never went short of food.

The children loved the open spaces. On Saturdays all the boys and girls from the neighbourhood met at their house to plan the day's activities. These involved all the children either walking and picnicking in the hills, catching tadpoles or swimming, depending on the season. Fishing and swimming picnics were regular events that all the family enjoyed.

If it is true that the pleasure of feeling good lies in the ability to express, then there on the farm those feelings were expressed to the fullest. There was laughter and fun, it was a joy to see and hear the children singing together, even Doris joined in. She spent a lot of time teaching them to appreciate the nature of the land they lived in. Doris still listened to music to keep her spirits up. She had her expectations and absolute faith that her husband would be a good provider. So far he proved to her that he was, but as a steady wage-earner she expected that he could improve their living standards. Sometimes she wondered whether it may have been better not to have had that expectation, then she would never be disappointed.

Gerry had no real ambition, he just drifted along with no real plans for the future. It was Doris who usually came up with ideas on how the family could achieve a better quality of life. Gerry was very talented and skilled with his hands. He loved working with wood and also took great pleasure in the fruit trees and vegetable garden he maintained. He would grab a handful of soil and watch it crumble back to the ground. He was a caring, loving father and a considerate husband.

Living out of town had its merits and it also had its problems, the greatest hardship was that there was no running water. Gerry had to cart it in a tank on the back of the truck to fill the rainwater tank attached to the house. But that didn't spoil the frugal yet contented life that Doris and her family enjoyed at Waggrakine. It was a small but lively community, which held regular dances at the local hall, and held an annual Christmas party that everyone looked forward to. These events gave Doris and her family the opportunity to socialise with their neighbours.

During the hot summer evenings the family would often sit on the sandy beach at Drummonds Cove and watch the sun set over the blue-green ocean. The sight filled Doris's heart with a sense of tranquillity.

Doris's days were taken up with the chores of homemaking and caring for her family. She liked to show off her skills in cooking whenever her husband's family visited them. Even his mother was impressed although her attitude towards Doris hadn't changed much. She only visited rarely and that's how Doris liked it.

Every week there were new adventures to experience and lessons to be learned, like the afternoon the schoolchildren found a huge melon in the field while taking a short cut home. The four took it in turns to roll it home. At first Doris thought it was a watermelon, but when she discovered that it was a pie melon she became very excited.

"I'll make some melon jam," she told her children, who were expecting to see a juicy watermelon. They were pleased to hear that their mother was making jam. They loved home-made jam, especially fig jam. They hadn't tasted melon jam, so they were looking forward to it.

She cleaned it up and, with a little bit of help from baby

Ricky, began the task of making jam. That afternoon she was pleased with the result. The jam seemed to be progressing nicely, but when she tasted it she was puzzled. It was as bitter as anything, so she added more sugar, but that didn't seem to sweeten it up at all. She gave up and waited until Gerry came home then told him about her dilemma. When he tasted the jam, he spat it out instantly.

"Yuk, that's not a pie melon, that's a bloody paddymelon," he said, laughing at the disappointed look on his wife's face. Doris took a last peek at the stuff in the large saucepan and thought to herself about all that sugar gone to waste.

"What happened to the jam, Mummy?" asked Sonny as all the rest gathered around with quizzical looks on their faces.

"It's no good, we have to throw it out," Doris replied. When she saw the disappointment in their little faces she told them she would make lots of fig jam for them later on. They seemed to be happy with that prospect, and ran off to play until tea time.

The children thrived and made excellent progress, and they continued to enjoy their regular outings to town. Time went by too quickly and soon the two eldest, Bernadine and Geraldine, were attending Geraldton Senior High School in town. For the family as a whole, the quality of life was unchanged and the years passed uneventfully until one afternoon while checking the mail Doris found an interest-ing-looking letter addressed to her husband. Doris waited patiently for him to return home from work.

It was a long-awaited letter from the State Housing inform-ing him that his family had been allocated a house in Bluff Point, close to everything. The jubilant family piled into the car straight away, everyone anxious to inspect their new four-bedroomed brick and tile home.

The move brought many changes, both positive and negative. Ricky, their youngest, started at the local primary school and the three eldest, Bernadine, Geraldine and Sonny, attended Geraldton Senior High School.

A few weeks after settling in her new home Doris was approached by the Community and Child Health Services to join the staff as a Nursing Aide. She accepted and it was a position she was to hold for four and a half years.

She worked in the local Yamatji community, helping to build an awareness of health problems in the home and explaining the services available, also encouraging the community to trust the health services. The hard work and the effectiveness of the community nurse helped lead to a reduction in the infant mortality rate.

It was during this time, while engrossed in her work and most days arriving home totally exhausted, that Doris began ignoring Gerry's negative attitude and hurtful comments towards her.

Then one day she received a phone call from the Community Health Sister at Jigalong. It was a call she was dreading as her father had been diagnosed with cancer of the pancreas six months earlier.

"Your father has just passed away," the solemn voice told her. The words took a second to sink in. "Are you all right, Doris?"

Doris didn't reply, instead she put her head on her desk and broke down crying. She was inconsolable. Her brother-in-law and co-worker, Paul, took her home where Gerry comforted her. Doris was once again deprived of her father's love, only this time it was forever.

The traditional funeral was a new experience and a first-time involvement for Doris. No one explained the proceedings; she was absolutely terrified. The burial rites were held in the dry sandy bed of the Jigalong River where the whole community was gathered in their appropriate kinship groups.

Doris was taken around and introduced to each group, each offering their respects. An aunt then led her by the hand to where the immediate family were rubbing their heads and upper bodies with a salve of red ochre and animal fat.

When her aunt told her to sit down on the tarpaulin with the family, she refused. In her youth she had to listen to words like "evil devil worshippers", and "heathen fornicators", which was the way traditional Aboriginal people were referred to when Doris was at the mission. She was frightened. Was this some sort of a Satanic ritual? She fought back images of the powers of darkness rising from the depths of Hell to join in the funeral rites.

But to her relief she learned this was an age-old ceremony that had been practiced for thousands of years and was still an important part of her people's culture. Amazed, she found after the funeral that she was able to talk about her father without breaking down.

Doris returned home but realised that the appeal and the challenge of her work had gone and that she had outgrown the health service. She needed new prospects, another challenge.

Meanwhile, the psychological and verbal abuse at home gathered momentum as the barbed words and accusations increased. Doris began to fear the smell or even the suggestion of alcohol and when Gerry was heavily intoxicated she avoided him by waiting until he was asleep before going to bed. She longed for peace, even if only in a good night's sleep.

Doris tried to conceal her true feelings from her children, but they were able to see beneath the disguise. They saw how their father was trying to destroy her by playing mind-control games. The games became more frequent and her self-esteem began falling. Her bouts of depression increased. There must be a way out of this awful situation, she told herself.

All her children except one — Ricky, the youngest — had left home. Doris had fulfilled the promise that she made to her unborn children when she was a teenager back on the mission at Roelands, and that was that they would grow up to know their parents. That solemn vow had been fulfilled.

After Gerry had graduated from the General Studies course at the Geraldton TAFE and had been accepted to do a special course in Perth, Doris believed that the change would be beneficial to her and Ricky. She was very happy about the move. Unfortunately it only compounded the problem. Gerry returned every semester break and these times that should have been times of joy and affection, proved to be dismal and unhappy because she was now being subjected to physical as well as emotional and verbal abuse.

Doris often wondered how a mild-mannered, modest man could change into a loud, obnoxious individual when under the influence of alcohol. This Jekyl-and-Hyde character was a total stranger. He was certainly not the man she'd fallen in love with, married and promised to stay with "until death do us part".

She recognised that the basis of their problems was that Gerry felt humiliated by the fact that he was dependent on a woman's income for financial support. As the wage earner and a hard worker since the age of fifteen this was intolerable; he was convinced that he had lost face, particularly in the Yamatji community around Geraldton.

It took one inexcusable night of excessive drinking and a violent attack to force Doris to make the decision about whether to remain a victim of her husband's instability.

Later, standing motionless in the stillness of the night, her face throbbing with pain, she looked up and saw the night sky lit by the bright silver moon. Her thoughts went back to the past when she had found comfort in the sacred songs that gave her inner peace and the courage to persevere. She began to sing silently, in her heart. It was a plea for help.

Pass me not, oh Gentle Saviour
Hear my humble cry,
While on others thou art calling,
Do not pass me by.

Saviour, Saviour, hear oh hear my humble cry;
And while on others thou art calling
Do not pass me by.

Thou art the spring of all my comfort
More than life to me,
Whom have I on earth beside Thee
Whom in heaven but Thee.

She paused for a moment and listened for her husband's snoring, then returned to the house quietly, so that she wouldn't wake him. She settled herself on the lounge and with some difficulty fell asleep. The next day when Bernadine and Geraldine came over for lunch they saw their mother's swollen face.

"You have to leave him, Mum."

"But what about Ricky? Who's going to look after him for me?" she asked her daughters.

"We will," Bernadine reassured her mother.

"I'll think about it," Doris promised them.

Late that afternoon, while sitting on the white sandy beach watching Ricky and one of his friends enjoying a game with the family pets, Doris told herself: "Now it's time for action."

As the sun was setting over the blue-green sea she sat watching one of the most beautiful sunsets she had ever seen. With the swift twilight came her decision, it was time to make a drastic change in her life. She had to make a fresh start somewhere else. Like her mother, Molly Kelly, she had the determination and the strength to confront any new challenge and, when spring returns, you can be sure that Doris Pilkington will once again be walking amongst beautiful wildflowers somewhere in this wonderful country of ours, celebrating the resurrection of life itself.

EPIGRAPH

The Healing Tree

TODAY, MORE THAN FIFTY YEARS since I was taken from the place of my birth, I have returned. It has taken lots of thought and courage to arrive at this exciting and moving point in my life. The pilgrimage to my birthplace has been a dream I've kept within my heart for many years.

I've left the city behind and come home to Jigalong, picked up my mother Molly, and headed for Balfour Downs to find my beginning, that actual wintamarra tree under which I was born. This wasn't my first attempt to find the wintamarra tree. In October 1991, on the fiftieth anniversary of our removal from the station, I pressured my mother to show me my birthplace. In my enthusiasm and eagerness I overlooked the most important factor — my mother's own emotional journey, and did absolutely nothing to minimise the trauma of reviving the past. As a result that visit was brief and I gained very little.

It was a late afternoon in May and the bloodwood trees cast long shadows on the sparsely populated red dry earth as we drove along. The monotony of the dryness and the black shiny gibber plains is relieved only by clumps of spinifex grass scattered over the flats right down to the deep rocky gullies and beyond. The silence and the wide, open spaces are something I have learned to appreciate. It is this landscape and the Pilbara people who live here that keep drawing me back time and time again.

The station homestead sat abandoned and the garden had been taken over by cattle. Everyone, the workers, the Dunnets, had moved on. It didn't take long for Mum to point out that very special spot where the wintamarra tree stands, close but distant enough from where the workers' camps once flourished.

Sitting under the wintamarra tree on Balfour Downs with my mother, she recalled the story of my birth. I'd left the station when I was only three-and-a-half years old, sent south with Mum and Anna because Mum needed surgery and there were no hospitals nearby that treated Aboriginal people. So Mum was sent to Royal Perth Hospital, while baby Anna and I were sent to Moore River Native Settlement. Mum believed that she would be coming home with both her children, but that wasn't to be.

At Moore River I was too small to understand why I was there. We weren't allowed to speak "blackfella language". We had no contact with Mardu people, who were then referred to as "full bloods". That was very difficult for me, because I grew up with my people, my father was Mardu, and I talked language. But at Moore River they belted it out of me.

Mardu people who spoke my traditional language were called "primitives" and "uncivilised". That was the beginning of the conditioning, the negative stereotyping against my own family. When the caste system was introduced they graded us like cattle. We were octoroons, with one eighth Aboriginal blood, or quarter-caste, or half-caste. Light-skinned children were conditioned to look down on their own people. The caste system caused a lot of trauma, right through to when they were adults, because they were discriminating against their own relations, their own brothers and sisters.

I didn't know I'd been taken from my mother. I just thought she'd left me there at Moore River, that she took me there herself and then went back to Jigalong. I thought she'd just handed me over to the Government. Mum didn't. I asked her years later, why did she hand me over to the Native Affairs? She broke down, she told me I'd been taken from her, that she had no rights as an Aboriginal mother, like so many others. If the Government wanted your children, you had no rights to prevent their removal. You just sat down to cry and mourn for your lost children. There was nothing else to do.

When the settlements were closing down in the late 1940s, and the Government was encouraging the establishment of Christian missions, I was sent to Roelands along with the other kids identified as Anglican at Moore River. Almost immediately the missionaries began trying to convert us; we were poor little sinners who needed to be saved. They were zealous in making us born-again Christians. They conditioned us to believe further negative stereotypes about our people, saying they were "evil" people, and when they practiced their traditional customs they were "devil worshippers".

At that time I didn't know much about my father — not till many years later — and I believed it all. So you can imagine the trauma I went through as an adult meeting my mother and dad. It took me ten years to actually sit down and start my journey of healing, which was necesssary for me to reconnect to my land and to reclaim my language and culture. It took ten years, because the conditioning was so strong that I had to metaphorically go through it all again, undo all that conditioning and come back.

Since then lots of things have happened. I've also become a published writer. I've written down the experiences of other people who've made their journey in search of their family histories in books like *Caprice, A Stockman's Daughter*, a fiction story based on some parts of my own life. *Caprice* has helped quite a few people, not just Indigenous women but others who suffered from domestic violence. *Caprice* gave them hope that there is a God out there, or something there who cares, and they only have to say: "I'm getting out of this situation", and start to break the pattern of domestic violence.

After that I was fortunate to hear my mother's story, and find the documents supporting it, from which I wrote *Follow the Rabbit-Proof Fence*. That story was a privilege given to me by Auntie Daisy and my mother, to be shared with everybody all throughout this country and indeed the world. The film of their story has highlighted the issue of the Stolen Generation and has encouraged other people to take the step forward on the journey of healing as the film goes around nationally and internationally. Non-Indigenous people will be aware of what we are saying, of what the Stolen Generation means to Aboriginal people. Not all of us are asking for compensation in terms of money, but what we need are support and recognition, and acceptance of our shared histories. We need to teach the children, break down the negative stereotypes so we can get on with enjoying our rights as other people do in this country. Justice — you just have to look around you to see the injustice in this country. We need equal rights and equal opportunities in the workplace, in education and all other aspects of life. I hope *Rabbit-Proof Fence* will encourage the movement towards understanding that and working together.

Anna was sent to Sister Kates in Perth when she was only two, and she had no contact with her mum. I've met her once, when I was at Royal Perth Hospital during my nursing aide course. It was like meeting just anybody, there was no embrace, nothing. We were miles apart, her attitude was different to mine, I suppose because of the environment she grew up in. She was given an altered vision of her history and I think she prefers that. I was angry at first, but now I'm very sympathetic towards her. I think: Little sister, we have a wonderful mother, our Jigalong family, and this absolutely beautiful country … this is our heritage and you're missing out.

* * *

I believe our spiritual side is developed later in life; spirituality is important to us Indigenous women. My spirituality became stronger after I had a breast cancer operation. Because my body was so traumatised by the removal of a special part of the body it took quite a few months to come to terms with that. For some Aboriginal people it's the same;

it takes a fair while to come to terms with what was missing from our lives.

The journey of healing and the healing process is similar to the wintamarra tree, my birthplace. When I was born here there was one tree, now, because over the years it died, four others have replaced it. This is in fact the story of life — you lose one part of your life and you get others coming through, stronger. This is a message I give to the members of the Stolen Generation, particularly the women. We all now need to develop our spirituality, this is making us stronger, and we're going to be the leaders of the movement to heal our people.

The wintamarra tree of my birthplace is a permanent reminder of the beginning of my life, and of the wonderful lady who gave birth to me here on the ground in the traditional way, so my connections to the land are very strong. The cycle will go on, like the family, the old people go and the younger ones come up. Although the tree at my birthplace is dead, the original tree, its roots are still there down in the earth, and four new trees have grown up. It's always been there, waiting for me to come and reconnect to my birthplace.

Glossary

Banaka	kinship group
binana	banana
Bududjara	people and language group of Western Desert region
bukala	quickly, hurry
bungarra	goanna
bunna	the ground, dirt
Burungu	kinship group
Buungul	traditional name for Rudall River area
cadgebut	thorny acacia tree
carrier	pregnant (Jigalong usage)
coolamon	a dish, also wirni
cousin-sister	kinship category, daughter of mother's sister or mother's kinship sister
dgudu	older sister
Dgududani	creation or dreaming stories
dguni	stomach

dogger   dingo shooter

Garimara   kinship group
Gilla/Jilla   people of Rudall River region
Gududjara   people and language group

Jilla   *see* Gilla
juma   grandfather (at Moore River)

kanyjamurra   bush yarn, root
kurrara   evergreen acacia shrub

Law Business   ceremonial rites and rituals of Mardu
                  people

Mandildjara   people and language group of Mardudjara
Mardu wangka   Aboriginal language in general
Mardu   *see* Mardudjara
Mardudjara   people and language group of Western
                  Desert region, includes Gududjara and
                  Mandildjara
marlbu   flesh-eating Spirit Being
marta   pass it to me, quickly
mata   wild sweet potatoes, yams
mayi   small damper made from spinifex or other
                  plant seeds
midka   eating
Millungga   kinship group
muda-muda   half-caste
murrundu   goanna

ngidi	youngest son, last child
Nyoongah	people of south-west of Western Australia
nguba	spouse
ngulu	taboo
numbi	woman's dance, part of marriage ceremony
pink-eye time	holiday time, summer
pula-pula	small lizards
umari	mother-in-law; mother-in-law song
unna	Isn't it so? Isn't that right?
wamula	bush tomatoes
wandi	a girl
wangka	to talk; Aboriginal language
wanna	umbilical cord
wirni	a dish, also coolamon
Wongi	people of Eastern Goldfields region
worrah worrah	wail of distress or fear
wudgebulla	white person
wuundu	shelters made from tree branches, or sheets of iron
yali	hot weather, summer
Yamatji	people of Meekatharra region
yardini	come here
yowada	horse

Black Australian Writing Series

Since 1988 with the establishment of the David Unaipon competition, which discovers new Aboriginal and Torres Strait Islander writers, UQP has built up an international reputation as the largest publisher of books by Indigenous authors in Australia. UQP's Black Australian Writing series evolved out of the Unaipon Award and today includes Indigenous-authored books ranging from novels, poetry, and life stories to nonfiction, and young adult fiction. Through the combined expertise of our authors, cultural advisors and specialist staff, UQP continues its commitment to Indigenous writing as a valued contribution to the literature of a nation.

Available in UQP's Black Australian Writing Series are:

DORIS PILKINGTON/NUGI GARIMARA
CAPRICE: A stockman's daughter

A fictional account of one woman's journey to find her family and heritage, *Caprice* is Doris Pilkington Garimara's first book. Set in the towns, pastoral stations and orphanage-styled institutions of Western Australia, this story brings together three generations of Mardu women. The narrator Kate begins her journey with the story of her grandmother Lucy, a domestic servant, then traces the short and tragic life of her mother Peggy.

Winner of the 1990 David Unaipon Award
ISBN 0 7022 3356 0
Fiction

DORIS PILKINGTON/NUGI GARIMARA
FOLLOW THE RABBIT-PROOF FENCE

'A marvellous adventure story and thriller, celebrating the courage and the resilience of the human heart.'

— Phillip Noyce, Director of 'Rabbit-Proof Fence'

This book is the basis of the internationally released film 'Rabbit-Proof Fence'. Based on her mother Molly's life story, Doris Pilkington Garimara's narrative tells of three young girls' remarkable journey home across the length of Western Australia.
ISBN 0 7022 3355 2
Non-fiction

VIVIENNE CLEVEN
HER SISTER'S EYE
Powerful and sinister, this is the second book by the brilliant Murri writer whose comedy novel *Bitin' Back* (2001) won the David Unaipon Award and was shortlisted in the 2002 South Australian Premier's Award for Fiction. Cleven's facility with noir is every bit as biting as her wit. *Her Sister's Eye* is a haunting descent into the tragedies of lives both black and white in a small town community with a legacy of shame.
ISBN 0 7022 3283 1
Fiction

VIVIENNE CLEVEN
BITIN' BACK
This is a rollicking comedy novel that blends in nimbly the realities of small town prejudice and racial intolerance. When football-playing Nevil awakens one morning determined to don a frock and "eyeshada" to better understand the late novelist Jean Rhys, his mother's idle days at the bingo hall are ended forever. Neither fist fights at the Two Dogs Pub, bare knuckle boxing in the back paddock, Booty's pig dogs or a police siege can slow the countdown on this human time bomb.
Winner of the 2000 David Unaipon Award
ISBN 0 7022 3249 1
Fiction

ROBERT LOWE
THE MISH
An award-winning story of family, community and tradition on Victoria's Framlingham Aboriginal Mission. *The Mish* is a charming, humorous memoir of times past, about growing up on western Victoria's Framlingham Aboriginal Station in the 1950s and '60s. Robert Lowe's family came to the Mission of their own volition at a time when mixed race marriages were better supported by the Aboriginal community than by the white community. A celebration of the resilient and unified extended family.
Winner of the 2001 David Unaipon Award
ISBN 0 7022 3327 7
Memoir

SAMUEL WAGAN WATSON
OF MUSE, MEANDERING AND MIDNIGHT
The youngest winner yet of the Unaipon Award, Samuel Wagan Watson is in demand for his songlike poems. This striking volume ranges widely from carefree youth to the pull of family and Murri community, and the bittersweet encounters of the heart. Ghosted by ancestors and muses,

Watson's cityscape interweaves past and present in a language that is playful, rhythmic and evocative.
Winner of the 1999 David Unaipon Award
ISBN 0 7022 3174 6
Poetry

SAMUEL WAGAN WATSON
ITINERANT BLUES
In his second book, Samuel Wagan Watson continues the neon night language of his debut collection *Of Muse, Meandering and Midnight* (2000). Set against his trademark industrial backdrop is the restless troubadour's slow burning and misspent passion. In a homegrown, Beat style, Watson takes to the road with his muse riding shotgun, looking for adventure.
ISBN 0 7022 3282 3
Poetry

RUTH HEGARTY
IS THAT YOU, RUTHIE?
Told with a vivid, entertaining and authentic voice, this is a unique account of a dormitory girl's life on the inside, at Queensland's notorious Cherbourg Aboriginal Mission in the 1930s. Murri elder Ruth Hegarty writes for every stolen child — and in the great cause of Reconciliation.
Winner of the 1998 David Unaipon Award
ISBN 0 7022 3099 5
Memoir

ALEXIS WRIGHT
PLAINS OF PROMISE
Vividly imagined, authentic in detail, with a forceful narrative and strong spiritual content this novel heralds the arrival of an outstanding Australian fiction writer.

"The Gulf Country ... is presented as a marvelous, magical landscape."

— Liam Davison

"Alexis Wright takes the Australian novel to places it has never been before."

— Jenny Pausacker

ISBN 0 7022 2917 2
Fiction